No Other Road to Take

(Không Còn Đường Nào Khác)
Memoir of Mrs. Nguyễn Thị Định

Mai V. Elliott, translator

No Other Road to Take
(Không Còn Đường Nào Khác)

Memoir of Mrs. Nguyễn Thị Định

Recorded by Trần Hương Nam

SOUTHEAST ASIA PROGRAM PUBLICATIONS
Southeast Asia Program
Cornell University
Ithaca, New York
1976

Cornell Southeast Asia Program Publications
640 Stewart Avenue, Ithaca, NY 14850-3857

Data Paper: Number 102

Printed in the United States of America

ISBN 978-0-877271-02-4

PREFACE

For most Westerners the origins and character of both the southern Việt Minh and the subsequent National Liberation Front (NLF) have remained largely a manner of speculation. However, the account that is here published provides some unusually deep insights into the hitherto obscure formative stages of the revolutionary movement in South Vietnam, particularly the beginnings of the NLF in one of the key provinces there in 1959-60. Centering on the political and military role of Mrs. Nguyễn Thị Định, a woman who became one of the NLF's most prominent leaders, this memoir also provides eloquent testimony to the important part played by women in Vietnam's post-war struggle for independence.

Born in 1920 in a peasant family in the Mekong delta province of Bến Tre, Nguyễn Thị Định joined the anti-French revolutionary movement when she was still in her teens. In 1938 she married a revolutionary friend of her brother's, but just after the birth of their son her husband was arrested by the French and deported to Poulo Condore. She herself was arrested in 1940 and sent to a prison camp. Following her release in 1943 she resumed her revolutionary activities, and in 1945 was one of the leaders of the Việt Minh's insurrection that seized power in Bến Tre province. Subsequently she was elected to the Executive Committee of the women's association of the province and became its representative in the Việt Minh Front Province Committee. In 1946 she served on a delegation sent to Hà Nội to report on the situation in the South and to obtain military supplies for the southern resistance. She then personally supervised the transport of a large shipment of weapons south, running it through a French naval blockade. In January 1960, she led the uprising in Bến Tre province against the Diệm regime that is so graphically described in the present account. Following the success of this uprising, she was appointed to the leadership committee of the NLF in Bến Tre province. In 1964 she became member of the Presidium of the NLF Central Committee, and the next year at the General Women's Congress of South Vietnam was elected Chairman of the South Vietnam Women's Liberation Association. Also in 1965 she was appointed Deputy Commander of the South Vietnam Liberation Armed Forces.

Mai Elliott has here provided an excellent translation of Mrs. Nguyễn Thị Định's memoirs. Mrs. Elliott's substantial and carefully researched introduction gives a background against which can be better appreciated both the general events referred to in this memoir and the modern political and military history of the province of Bến Tre, upon which the account is primarily focused.

George McT. Kahin
January 21, 1976

Mrs. Nguyễn Thị Định,
Deputy Commander of the NLF Armed Forces

Mrs. Nguyễn Thị Định observing a female guerrilla unit in training

Mrs. Nguyễn Thị Định visiting an NLF unit

National Liberation Front Administrative and Military Subdivisions of South Vietnam

TRANSLATOR'S INTRODUCTION

BACKGROUND

Bến Tre province where Mrs. Nguyễn Thị Định was born is formed by three islands—Cù Lao Minh, Cù Lao Bảo, and Cù Lao An Hóa—separated from each other by branches of the Mekong River as it pours into the South China Sea. The islands are about sixty km in length; Cù Lao Bảo, the largest, at its widest point, measures about twelve km in width; while Cù Lao Minh measures from five to seven km in width; and Cù Lao An Hóa, the smallest of the three, is only a few kilometers wide. To the North, Bến Tre borders on Mỹ Tho province and to the South on Trà Vinh province. The islands are crisscrossed with canals and arroyos, and the main mode of transportation is by water. Bến Tre has rich alluvial soil which yields good crops of coconuts, rice, and fruit. The province is especially well known for its vast coconut groves which provide the main income for the islands. The numerous waterways and the sea are also a rich source of shrimp, crabs, fish, and other seafood. Besides its coconut products, Bến Tre is also well known for tobacco (which is grown in Mỏ Cày) and for the silk fabrics of Ba Tri where villagers breed silk worms.[1]

Administratively, the province is divided into nine districts (Trúc Giang, Ba Tri, Thạnh Phú, Hàm Long, Bình Đại, Mỏ Cày, Giồng Trôm, Hương Mỹ, and Đôn Nhơn) and 115 villages.[2] The majority of the 500,000 inhabitants of the islands belong to the Buddhist faith. The Cao Đài form the second largest religious group with 100,000 adherents, followed by the Catholics who comprise 10 percent of the population, and by the Hòa Hảo who constitute the smallest religious community on the islands.[3]

Bến Tre is a province known for its revolutionary tradition (*truyền thống cách mạng*). Nguyễn Đình Chiểu, the foremost scholar of the South in the nineteenth century—whose literary masterpiece in verse, *Lục Vân Tiên*, is loved by all

---

[1] "Những hòn đảo xanh" (The Green Islands), *Thống Nhất* (March 29, 1963), and Xuân Vũ, *Bến Tre anh dũng* (Heroic Bến Tre) (Hà Nội: Phổ Thông, 1963).

[2] This is the administrative division adopted by the Sài Gòn government after 1954. Huỳnh Minh, *Địa linh nhân kiệt: Kiến Hòa xưa và nay* (Kiến Hòa province: Before and Now) (Gia Định: Published by Author, 1965). Bến Tre province was renamed Kiến Hòa province by the Ngô Đình Diệm government.

[3] "Những hòn đảo xanh" and *Bến Tre anh dũng*. These are old statistics. No new ones are available. The data on the Catholics is from Jean Leroy, *Un homme dans la rizière* (Paris: Editions de Paris, 1955), p. 120.

Southerners—retreated to this province to teach after the French had occupied his native province of Gia Định and Cần Giuộc where he had fled after the fall of Gia Định in 1859. *Đồ Chiểu* (Scholar Chiểu) as he was popularly known refused to collaborate with the French in spite of their repeated efforts to entice him with material benefits. While in Bến Tre, he was in contact with the two most famous anti-French resistance leaders of the period, Đốc binh Là and Trương Công Định, and composed his large body of patriotic poems which were quickly spread among the population.[4]

After the French conquest of the Mekong Delta provinces in June 1867,[5] several uprisings occurred in Bến Tre. The most serious challenge to the French in the province was led by two sons of the patriot Phan Thanh Giản,[6] Phan Tôn and Phan Thanh Liêm. They commanded an army of 40,000 men (*nghĩa quân*, or "army fighting for a just cause"), and their resistance spread to all of Western Nam Bộ (Western South Việt Nam), with the strongest centers being in Bến Tre, Trà Vinh, and Vĩnh Long provinces. Their biggest attack took place in November 1867 in Hương Điểm, Bến Tre province, and lasted for three days. The uprising then spread to the entire province with French posts manned by local recruits coming under the attack of the guerrillas.[7]

Another noteworthy uprising occurred in Mỏ Cày district (later the scene of the first "concerted uprising" in 1960) in the latter part of the nineteenth century. Its two leaders were subsequently captured by the French and deported to Reunion Island.[8] In the early part of the twentieth century, many anti-French movements found a sizable following in Bến Tre province—such as the Đông Du movement, supported by Phan Bội Châu, which encouraged young Vietnamese to go to Japan to study how to modernize Việt Nam in order to enable the country to cope with French domination; the *Thiên Địa Hội* [9] (Heaven and Earth) Association which triggered

---

[4] Xuân Vũ, *Bến Tre anh dũng*.

[5] The Huế Court was forced to cede the three provinces of Biên Hòa, Gia Định, and Định Tường to the French in 1862. The French conquered the remaining provinces in the Mekong Delta in June 1867.

[6] Phan Thanh Giản was the imperial envoy in charge of administering the six provinces of the Mekong Delta at the time of the French conquest in 1867. Feeling that he had failed in his mission to protect the six provinces against French occupation, he took poison and killed himself.

[7] Xuân Vũ, *Bến Tre anh dũng*, pp. 12-13.

[8] "Bến Tre bất khuất" (Indomitable Bến Tre), *Thống Nhất* (March 29, 1963).

[9] Ibid. The Thiên Địa Hội was a secret society in Southern China with the avowed aim of overthrowing the Manchu dynasty and restoring the Ming dynasty. It was brought to South Việt Nam by Chinese immigrants. However, the branches of the society which were transplanted in South Việt Nam lost their political contents, became mere societies for mutual protection, or degenerated into gangster societies engaged in extortion. The Vietnamese borrowed the organizational form of the Chinese Thiên Địa Hội, adopted some of their rituals, symbols, and secret signals, but added a political content to the association and transformed it into an anti-French movement. Its recruits came from the peasants, urban poor, and small landowners. The members of the association believed in the coming of a Living Buddha (*Phật sống*) who would be none other than a descendant of Emperor Hàm Nghi, whom the French had deported for his opposition to their domination. They were extremely brave in combat, believing that the talismans they wore would protect them from harm. Information compiled from Sơn Nam, *Thiên Địa Hội và cuộc Minh Tân* (The 'Heaven and Earth Society' and the 'Enlightenment and Modernization' Movement) (Sài Gòn: Phù Sa, 1971).

an uprising in Ba Vát in 1916; and the Thanh Niên movement in the 1920s, which was the nucleus of the future Indochinese Communist Party.[10]

THE VIỆT MINH AND THE RESISTANCE AGAINST THE FRENCH

After its formation in 1930, the Indochinese Communist Party (ICP) began to organize and recruit in Bến Tre province. Under its leadership, demonstrations broke out in many villages and districts of the province in 1930-31, during which several people were killed and many were wounded. The French retaliated by arresting over a thousand people, of whom 150 were thrown in prison and many of them were later deported to Poulo Condore (Côn Sơn prison island). Among those jailed was the ICP Province Party Committee Secretary.[11] French repression and arrests caused the ICP Province Party Committee to disintegrate in 1933, but the Party structure at the local levels survived and continued to operate as before. In 1935, the Bến Tre Province Party Committee was re-established and revolutionary activities expanded. In 1939-40, Bến Tre took part in making preparations for the *Nam Kỳ Khởi Nghĩa* (Southern Insurrection) which was then being planned by the ICP leadership in the South. However, due to internal betrayal the effort failed and many Province Party Committee members were arrested or killed. French repression in the wake of the Southern Insurrection of 1940 was extremely severe.[12]

The Province Party Committee was reconsolidated at the beginning of 1944. On August 25, 1945 the revolution seized power in Bến Tre province which remained a free zone for five months while the French concentrated their efforts on recapturing Sài Gòn-Chợ Lớn and the provinces around the capital area. After the French had reoccupied the provinces of Vĩnh Long, Mỹ Tho, and Trà Vinh, Bến Tre found itself surrounded on all sides. On February 7, 1946 the French launched a large scale assault with naval, air, and land forces. The Việt Minh troops in Bến Tre were outnumbered and outgunned. Their weapons at that time consisted of a couple of rifles and a few Japanese water mines that they had retrieved from the river.[13] To block the advance of French forces, roads were cut and trees were felled to make barricades.

The best known Việt Minh guerrilla commander of the period in Bến Tre province was Đồng Văn Cống (now holding the rank of general in the PRG) who ultimately built up his small unit, recruited at first among his own relatives, into the famous 99th Regiment. His initial followers started by seizing a post in 1946 and capturing two rifles. With this meager capital, they began to ambush small bands of soldiers to seize more weapons. Their equipment gradually grew to include submachine guns, machine guns, and mortars, all captured from the French. The unit

---

[10] "Bến Tre bất khuất," *Thống Nhất* (March 29, 1963).

[11] Ibid.

[12] The insurrection broke out in November 1940 in the provinces of Gia Định, Chợ Lớn, Tân An, Mỹ Tho, Cần Thơ, Vĩnh Long, Sóc Trăng, and Bạc Liêu, under the direction of the South Việt Nam Region Party Committee (Xứ Ủy Nam Kỳ). This insurrection triggered an exceptionally savage repression by the French colonial authorities which decimated Party organizations in the South. Rebel areas were bombed, thousands of people were arrested, over one hundred cadres were executed, and countless others were sent to Côn Sơn island.

[13] Xuân Vũ, *Bến Tre anh dũng.*

expanded and within a year became a well-equipped company, and then a regiment. This regiment was awarded the title "Model Regiment" by the South Vietnam Resistance Committee in 1947.[14]

In July 1947, General de la Tour, the French commander in the South, appointed Jean Leroy, a French officer of mixed Vietnamese and French blood and a native of Bến Tre province, to form three mobile brigades of Cao Đài adherents for the protection of the sector of Bình Đại in Bến Tre province that Leroy had cleared. Fearing that the introduction of Cao Đài soldiers into this mainly Catholic area would provoke a hostile popular reaction, Leroy proposed and obtained permission to form three Catholic brigades recruited locally.[15] Leroy called these units "Brigades catholiques," adopted the cross as their symbol and assigned them the motto, "Pro Deo et Patria" *(Vì Chúa Vì Tổ Quốc)*. This had all the tenets of a religious crusade and alarmed the Catholic Church in the South which was then maintaining a neutral position toward the Việt Minh. The Church protested, and Leroy was pressured to change the name of his brigades. He settled on the name "Unités mobiles de défense des Chrétientés" (Mobile Units for the Defense of Christian Communities), or UMDC for short.[16] After the Vatican issued its condemnation of Communism, however, the Catholic Church changed its attitude and began to provide moral support to the UMDC.[17]

Later, Leroy was authorized to create more brigades and, eventually, was in command of an army of 12,000, composed almost entirely of Catholics. The bulk of this army was stationed in Bến Tre province. In 1949, Leroy was named "Chef de Bataillon des Forces Suppletives" and "Inspecteur des UMDC," and given the prerogatives of a "Chef de Corps," with complete authority over the brigades under his command with regard to their recruitment, promotion, discipline, transfer, and training. Then his military power was reinforced with his appointment as Bến Tre Province Chief, thus giving him complete authority over both military and civilian matters in the province.[18]

Leroy ruled Bến Tre like his own fiefdom, in a highly autocratic manner and, in his ambition to transform Bến Tre into a "model province," proceeded to pacify it by using extremely ruthless means.[19] The Việt Minh accused him and his troops of

---

[14] Ibid., pp. 18-19. This method of attacking enemy troops and seizing their weapons to arm the revolutionary units was later applied with great success by the National Liberation Front at the start of the insurgency in the South in 1959-60.

[15] Leroy, *Un homme dan la rizière*, p. 120, and A. M. Savani, *Visage et images du Sud-Vietnam* (Saigon: n.p., 1953), p. 124.

[16] Though this still had a definite religious crusade ring to it, the name was found acceptable by the Church. The Vietnamese called the UMDC, the *uống máu dân chúng* ("Drinking the People's Blood"), because of their ruthless tactics in suppressing the revolution. See Xuân Vũ, *Bến Tre anh dũng*.

[17] A. M. Savani, *Visage et images du Sud-Vietnam,* p. 127.

[18] Ibid., p. 126. See also Jean Leroy, *Un homme dans la rizière*, pp. 141-142.

[19] Later, during the Second Indochina War, successive governments in Sài Gòn also tried to pacify Bến Tre province. Because of its reputation as a revolutionary stronghold, Bến Tre was subjected to intensive shellings, bombing, defoliation, and land operations, which caused heavy damage in lives and property to the people of this once prosperous province. Two officials of the Sài Gòn government made their reputation from their tenure as province chiefs of Bến Tre, considered the most "rotten" province in the Mekong Delta. They were Colonel Phạm Ngọc Thảo, who was Bến Tre province chief in 1962, and Trần Ngọc Châu, who was province chief from 1962 to 1963, and again from 1964 to 1965. Phạm Ngọc Thảo was later killed after an

many atrocities, such as the slaughter of village youths in Phước Thạnh village,[20] the murder of three hundred people in Cầu Hòa, and numerous killings in Nhơn Thạnh.[21] The brutality with which Leroy pacified the province was confirmed by a 1972 retrospective official Sài Gòn assessment:

> . . . Leroy applied an extremely rigid and firm pacification policy and acted in accordance with the principle of "an iron hand in a velvet glove." He did not hesitate to resort to brutal and indiscriminate killings, without distinguishing between friends and enemies. If Việt Minh clandestine activities, terrorism and assassinations occurred anywhere, the area concerned was immediately subjected to reprisals, and innocent civilians had to pay the price.[22]

In his memoir, Leroy claimed he succeeded in winning the people's allegiance with his reform program and cited impressive statistics (which cannot be verified elsewhere) to buttress his claim. He opened schools, built maternity clinics, health stations, and markets; forced landowners to reduce their rent from fifty *giạ* (about

---

attempted coup d'état in 1965. Trần Ngọc Châu who was elected to the National Assembly in 1968 was arrested and jailed by President Thiệu in 1970, in spite of his parliamentary immunity, because he opposed Thiệu's policies. The most disastrous pacification drive was carried out by the US Ninth Division in the latter part of 1968. This operation, called "Speedy Express," inflicted the worst destruction and killing on Bến Tre (then called Kiến Hòa province). According to Kevin Buckley, a *Newsweek* correspondent who did an intensive study of the operation: " . . . a staggering number of noncombatant civilians—perhaps as many as five thousand according to one official—were killed by US firepower to 'pacify' Kiến Hòa. . . . The Ninth Division put all it had into the operation. Eight thousand infantrymen scoured the heavily populated countryside, but contact with the elusive enemy was rare. Thus, in its pursuit of pacification, the division relied heavily on its fifty artillery pieces, fifty helicopters (many armed with rockets and mini-guns), and the deadly support lent by the Air Force. There were 3,381 tactical air strikes by fighter bombers during 'Speedy Express.' . . . Cumulative statistics for 'Speedy Express' show that 10,899 'enemy' were killed. In the month of March alone, 'over 3,000 enemy troops were killed . . . which is the largest monthly total for any American division in the Vietnam war,' said the division's official magazine. . . . The enormous discrepancy between body count [11,000] and the number of captured weapons [748] is hard to explain—except by the conclusion that many victims were unarmed innocent civilians . . ." The Vietnamese whom Buckley talked to confirmed that many of those "enemy" killed were actually farmers "gunned down while they were working in their rice fields." "Pacification's Deadly Price," *Newsweek* (June 19, 1972). The province was also heavily damaged in the American-Vietnamese counterattack during the Tết Offensive of 1968, during which Bến Tre Province Capital was completely leveled by bombing. Questioned about the destruction of this town, the American commander of the operation made the classic statement: "We had to destroy it to save it."

[20] "Bến Tre bất khuất," *Thống Nhất* (March 26, 1963).

[21] Xuân Vũ, *Bến Tre anh dũng*, p. 22. Later, after Leroy had been transferred elsewhere, many of his soldiers were tried by the Vietnamese government for their criminal behavior. Leroy ascribed this, however, to the power conflict between the civilian province chief and the military commander of the brigades who had been appointed to replace him. See *Un homme dans la rizière*, pp. 161-162.

[22] Bộ Tổng Tham Mưu and Khối Quân Sự, *Quân Lực Việt-Nam Cộng-Hòa trong giai đoạn hình thành* (Sài Gòn: Bộ Tổng Tham Mưu, 1972), p. 274, and Joint General Staff of the Army of the Republic of Vietnam, Military History Section, *The Formation of the Army of the Republic of Vietnam* (Saigon: Joint General Staff, 1972).

forty liters) per hectare to twenty *giạ*;[23] and threatened to use force against those who refused to comply. By 1952, the province was pacified and became the showcase for visiting dignitaries and journalists. However, the success was illusory. The province remained quiescent because of Leroy's ruthless and effective control apparatus and because of the extensive network of posts and the large force he maintained to keep things in check. The ephemeral nature of his pacification became apparent when the Việt Minh made a strong comeback six months after his transfer to another command.[24]

For the Việt Minh, the years 1948-1952 represented the most difficult period for their movement in Bến Tre province. When Leroy stepped up his attacks in 1948-1949, Việt Minh cadres had to flee from the province. However, they began to slip back afterward, despite the constant danger of detection and arrest. Leroy by this time had built an extensive network of posts to maintain security.[25] The period from 1950 to 1951 was a particularly difficult one. The province leadership committee was reduced to a mere handful of cadres living in a swampy area flooded with salt water and being supplied with provisions only once every five or six days.[26]

In November 1952, Leroy was summoned by General Bondis, then French commander in South Việt Nam, and asked to take charge of what the French called the Old Provinces (consisting of Bến Tre, Gò Công, Tân An, and parts of Mỹ Tho and Chợ Lớn) in the name of the Vietnamese National Army which the French were building up as part of their Vietnamization program to replace French forces. In order to get the budget for Indochina for that year passed by the National Assembly in Paris, the French command in Việt Nam wanted to show that the relief of French forces was proceeding satisfactorily, by presenting proof that command of the Old Provinces had passed to the Vietnamese government.[27] President Nguyễn Văn Tâm, who disliked the sects of the South and considered Leroy's UMDC a private religious army, was determined to dissolve his fief. Civilian and military authority in Bến Tre was split and no longer concentrated in the hands of one man, as had been the case with Leroy. According to Leroy, this led to an intense antagonism between the province chief and the military commander of the province, with the province chief eventually winning with the support of powerful ex-mandarins and landlords who wanted to reinstitute the old exploitative rents.[28] Leroy's UMDC was attached to the Vietnamese Army and then disbanded in May 1953. Leroy himself was shipped to France in April 1953 to attend courses at the Ecole superieure de guerre.[29]

In his memoir, Leroy said that security conditions deteriorated rapidly after

---

[23] Though his rent reduction program was considered quite daring by the landlords in the province at the time, the peasants who had had to pay *no* rent during the time the Việt Minh controlled the province must have looked upon it as a regressive measure.

[24] Leroy, *Un homme dans la rizière*, p. 162.

[25] Leroy said that one year after his arrival on the scene, the number of posts was raised from ninety-eight to 564. Ibid., p. 149.

[26] Xuân Vũ, *Bến Tre anh dũng*, p. 26.

[27] Leroy, *Un homme dans la rizière*, p. 160.

[28] According to Leroy, the peasants were forced to pay the old rent of fifty *giạ* per hectare, and the province chief even loaned his militia to the landlords, in exchange for huge bribes, to help them collect rents from the peasants or to repossess their land. Ibid., p. 164.

[29] Ibid., p. 166.

his transfer, and the reinstitution of the old exploitative system and corrupt practices alienated the peasants. If this were true, these factors probably did contribute to the renaissance of the Việt Minh in the province, but in actuality the quiescence during his tenure was deceptive and was due mainly to the oppressive control and fierce repression that he could exert. Though the Việt Minh were reduced to a small number of cadres and guerrillas, they managed to survive throughout this period, and this indicates that they must have enjoyed popular support. Though the main force of the Việt Minh had been pushed out of the province, they remained in the Plain of Reeds nearby and could come back when conditions permitted, as was the case in 1953. In that year, small Việt Minh attacks began to take place which culminated in an offensive in 1954 during which many posts in the province had to be abandoned by the Sài Gòn administration. The offensive was gaining momentum when it had to be halted by the Geneva cease-fire order.[30] At the time of the armistice, the Việt Minh controlled all of the province except its capital.[31]

THE POLICIES OF NGÔ ĐÌNH DIỆM

In compliance with the Geneva Agreements of 1954, Việt Minh soldiers in South Việt Nam regrouped to the North, and only a small number of cadres were left behind. According to the *Pentagon Papers*:

> A reported 90,000 soldiers were taken to North Việt Nam in the evacuated units, while the US and the GVN [Government of (South) Vietnam] estimated that 5,000 to 10,000 trained men were left behind as "cadre." If French estimates are correct that in 1954 the Việt Minh controlled over 60 to 90 percent of South Việt Nam's villages outside the Cao Đài and Hòa Hảo regions, those 5,000 to 10,000 cadre must have represented only a small fraction of the remaining Việt Minh apparatus—cadre, local workers, sympathizers—in the countryside.[32]

A number of those who stayed behind were assigned to carry out political activities, and prepare for the general elections scheduled for 1956 to reunify Việt Nam, as stipulated in the Geneva Agreements, while the others were simply told to return home and await further instructions. "It is quite clear that even the activists were not instructed to organize units for guerrilla war, but rather to agitate politically for the promised Geneva elections, and the normalization of relations with the North."[33] The Việt Minh at the beginning were confident that President Diệm would carry out the clauses of the accords. However, in January 1955 Diệm publicly repudiated them and then in clear violation of the amnesty clause of the Geneva Accords, launched the *Tố Cộng* ("Denunciation of Communists") campaign to liquidate the remnants of the Việt Minh and their sympathizers. It was this persecution and other unpopular policy measures—such

---

[30] Xuân Vũ, *Bến Tre anh dũng*, p. 27.

[31] Leroy, *Un homme dans la rizière*, p. 174.

[32] *The Pentagon Papers*, Senator Gravel Edition, Vol. I (Boston: Beacon Press, 1971), p. 328.

[33] Ibid.

as forcible population relocation, oppressive population control, the upsetting of agrarian relationships in the countryside, and the corruption and ruthlessness of his officials—that drove former Việt Minh resistants and the peasants to open revolt.

THE TỐ CỘNG CAMPAIGN

Initiated in the summer of 1955, this campaign was designed to force former members of the anti-French resistance and their sympathizers to surrender and repent their past actions in the Việt Minh movement, and denounce and reject communism at public ceremonies. Afterward they were forced to attend indoctrination courses at reeducation centers. Those who refused to go along, on the grounds that their participation in the resistance against the French to win national independence was not a crime and therefore required no public confession and repentance, were arrested, jailed, tortured, or simply liquidated.

In January 1956, Diệm intensified the tempo of the campaign by issuing a Presidential Ordinance which expanded the existing system of reeducation centers and authorized "the arrest and detention of anyone deemed dangerous to the safety of the state and their incarceration in one of several concentration camps."[34] In May 1959, the GVN promulgated Law 10/59 which "stiffened penalties for communist affiliations and permitted trial of accused by special military tribunals."[35] Death sentences were meted out to many of those arrested, and the guillotine—the hated symbol of French colonial repression—was hauled out for public executions to intimidate the people. The *Tố Cộng* campaign was stepped up in 1959 and:

> In 1960, a GVN Ministry of Information release stated that 48,250 persons had been jailed between 1954 and 1960, but a French observer estimates the numbers in jail at the end of 1956 alone at 50,000. P. J. Honey, who was invited by Diệm to investigate certain of the reeducation centers in 1959, reported that on the basis of his talks with former inmates, "the consensus of the opinions expressed by these people is that . . . the majority of the detainees are neither communists nor pro-communists."[36]

The hunt for Việt Minh cadres and their sympathizers was carried out in the urban areas as well, but it was in the countryside that it was pushed most energetically. Former members of the Resistance enjoyed great prestige among the population for their participation in the fight against the French, and their blanket condemnation and the indiscriminate persecution of ordinary peasants as sympathizers of the Việt Minh caused widespread popular resentment. In the view of the analysts of the *Pentagon Papers*, "Whatever it contributed to GVN internal security . . . the Communist Denunciation Campaign thoroughly terrified the Vietnamese peasants. . . ."[37]

---

[34] Ibid., p. 311.

[35] Ibid.

[36] Ibid.

[37] Ibid., p. 255.

POPULATION CONTROL

To ensure better control of the population and prevent communist penetration of the countryside, Ngô Đình Diệm also instituted police measures which the peasants found extremely irksome and threatening. Families were organized into *liên gia* or inter-family groups of between three and five families each. A similar number of *liên gia* formed a *khóm*, and each *liên gia* and *khóm* were headed by a chief who had to report to the government on the behavior and activities of people under his control, and pass down government orders to the people. "Each *liên gia* was held responsible for the political behavior of its members and was expected to report suspicious behavior (the presence of strangers, unusual departures, and like events)."[38] In addition, each household was required to post a board outside their home, listing the number, age, and sex of each of their members. The *liên gia* system in fact required the peasants to spy on one another for the benefits of a government that they disliked.

The police identification system was also made more effective, each adult being fingerprinted and issued an identity card which he was required to carry at all times. The population was classified into different categories, depending on what the GVN authorities judged was the degree of their sympathy for the Việt Minh. Often, this classification was quite arbitrary and caused deep resentment. Those who were issued ID cards with letters placing them in unfavorable categories were frequently harassed by the local officials and police, either because they distrusted them or wanted to extort money from them.

LAND REFORM

American officials in Việt Nam —well aware that unless Diệm could win the support of the peasantry all the security measures he adopted would prove ineffective against communist infiltration of the countryside—prodded him to initiate a land reform program to correct a situation wherein in 1954 "one quarter of 1 percent of the population owned 40 percent of the rice growing land."[39] However, the result of this land reform was simply to disrupt the land pattern that had been established by the Việt Minh during the Resistance period, and this *xáo canh* (disruption of land pattern) was one of the main factors which bred popular

---

[38] Ibid., p. 312.

[39] Ibid., p. 309. According to Robert Scigliano, at first ". . . the government resisted American pressures for land transfer and effective rent control programs, 'not wishing to disturb the strong landowning classes'. Action was produced only after General J. Lawton Collins, President Eisenhower's special ambassador, was dispatched to Sài Gòn in November, 1954, with instructions that reportedly stipulated effective agrarian reform as a condition of the increased American aid which President Diệm was seeking." Robert Scigliano, *South Vietnam: Nation Under Stress* (Boston: Houghton Mifflin Company, 1963), p. 121. In their study of this period, George McT. Kahin and John W. Lewis said that, "When at American urging, Diệm finally introduced a program of land distribution, this was both in scope and actual practice far less than US officials had proposed. The funds allocated for it were grossly inadequate, and a considerable part was diverted for the financing of security programs. In its implementation, the program was so emasculated and rigged in favor of the landlords that it tended to inflame rather than diminish the peasant's hostillty." *The United States in Vietnam* (New York: Delta, 1967), p. 105.

discontent. Under the GVN land reform program (which did not really get under way until the beginning of 1958), individual land holdings in excess of 284 acres (still a sizable holding)[40] would be expropriated and resold to tenant farmers. This "maximum retainable by individual owners left only about 20 percent of the total cultivated rice area, or about 1.2 million acres eligible for transfer."[41] Also, beginning in 1957, the GVN attempted to regulate landlord-tenant relations by fixing rents at 15-25 percent of the crop yield and guaranteeing tenant tenure for three to five years (through landlord-tenant contracts) to prevent arbitrary evictions by landlords. The net effect of this measure—which was in any case not fully implemented—was to impress on the farmers that the land which the Việt Minh had distributed to them free of charge was now irrevocably restituted to the landlords whose ownership rights were recognized by GVN laws.[42]

The land expropriated from the landlords was not redistributed free but was simply available for purchase to the tenants through payments in installments to the government. However, they only obtained title to it after paying for the land in full.[43] Since the Việt Minh had given them ownership of the land during the Resistance, the peasants "naturally resented having to purchase what they already regarded as their own."[44] In many instances, however, landlords escaped expropriation by transferring titles to their relatives.[45] During the Resistance years, a large number of these landlords had fled to the urban areas to escape Việt Minh reprisals, but now with the reestablishment of Sài Gòn control, they came back to reclaim their land and collect rents, usually with the connivance and assistance of local officials who placed the militia at their disposal for these purposes. In addition, many landlords ignored the Sài Gòn government's injunction against excessive rents, and forced tenants to pay more than the maximum allowance rent of 25 percent of the annual crop yield—sometimes as high as twice that amount.[46] In the view of the authors of the *Pentagon Papers*:

Tenant farmers were . . . disaffected, for . . . many farmers, after eight or so rent-

---

[40] According to Jeffrey Race, "By comparison, Japan, Korea, and Taiwan, which also carried out extensive postwar land reforms, limited retention to only three to four hectares. Considerable leeway was also allowed to landlords to minimize or escape the impact of expropriation: the additional allowance of fifteen hectares for ancestor worship; the right to keep lands converted to industrial crops; the right to select and retain the best land. Finally, the beneficiaries of the program were required to repay the government on harsher terms than those the government allowed the expropriated landlords." *War Comes to Long An* (Berkeley: University of California Press, 1972), pp. 58-59.

[41] Scigliano, *South Vietnam: Nation Under Stress*, p. 122. Even absentee landlords were allowed to retain this maximum amount of rice land. Kahin and Lewis, *The United States in Vietnam*, p. 105.

[42] Race, *War Comes to Long An,* p. 91.

[43] Kahin and Lewis, p. 105. Because of bureaucratic red-tape only a small number of peasants actually got title to the land available for purchase. According to Jeffrey Race's survey of the situation in Long An province, "Of the 7,370 hectares of expropriated land, 5,022 hectares were finally surveyed; 3,613 people filed applications for purchase. Only 973 titles were returned from Sài Gòn by 1960, and none in 1961." *War Comes to Long An*, p. 59.

[44] Kahin and Lewis, *The United States in Vietnam*, p. 105.

[45] Robert L. Sanson, *The Economics of Insurgency in the Mekong Delta* (Cambridge: MIT Press, 1970), p. 58.

[46] Ibid., p. 57.

free years, could see no justice in resuming payments to a long absent owner particularly since the Việt Minh had assured them the land was their by right.[47]

The implementation of the land reform program was inevitably accompanied by abuses, and in addition "agrarian courts" which were "established to settle landlord-tenant disputes soon came under the domination of landlords and officials friendly to them, to the obvious disadvantage of the ordinary peasants."[48]

Modest in scope and half-hearted as Diệm's land reform was, compared to the one carried out by the Việt Minh during the Resistance, it encountered fierce opposition from the landlords and their supporters within the administration. As a result, the program was not actively pushed by the officials and ministries concerned. However, according to the *Pentagon Papers:*

> . . . even if the goals of the program had been honestly fulfilled—which they were not—only 20 percent of rice land would have passed from large to small farmers. Ultimately only 10 percent of all tenant farmers benefited. . . . As it happened . . . the distribution program was not only of limited scope, but, by 1958 or 1959, it was virtually inoperative. Bernard Fall has reported that despite Diệm's land reform, 45 percent of the land remained concentrated in the hands of 2 percent of landowners, and 75 percent in the hands of 15 percent.[49]

Far from winning the allegiance and support of the peasants, the GVN land reform program only succeeded in alienating them further from the Sài Gòn regime.

POPULATION RELOCATION

To enhance security further in the countryside, Diệm decided to relocate the peasants in easily defensible settlements where they could also be more effectively watched. The relocation began in February 1959 in areas of Western Nam Bộ which had been under strong Việt Minh control during the Resistance. There were two types of centers: one for families with relatives who had regrouped to the North, and the other for villagers whom the Sài Gòn government considered its loyal supporters. "Peasants were transported from their rice fields, they were expected to reestablish their lives with minimal assistance from the government. The reaction of both loyal and 'Communist-contaminated' peasants was unanimously bitter, and the hastily conceived program was suspended about March 1959."[50] Then in July 1959, a new population relocation program was adopted:

> . . . Diệm announced that the GVN was undertaking to improve rural standards

---

[47] *The Pentagon Papers*, Vol. I, p. 309.

[48] Kahin and Lewis, *The United States in Vietnam*, p. 103.

[49] *The Pentagon Papers*, Vol. I, p. 309. According to Scigliano, "There were 1,584 landowners expropriated and 111 thousand benefiting peasant households, most of them tenants. In short, of an estimated 1 to 1.2 million tenant households existing in 1955, only 10 percent obtained land under the government's land transfer program." *South Vietnam: Nation Under Stress*, p. 123.

[50] Ibid., p. 179.

of living through establishing some 80 "prosperity and density centers" *(khu trù mật).* These "agrovilles" were to be located along a "strategic route system"—key roads, protected by new towns. Some 80 agrovilles were to be built by the end of 1963, each designed for 400 families (2,000 to 3,000 people), and each with a surrounding cluster of smaller agrovilles for 120 families. The GVN master plan provided for each community defense, schools, dispensary, market center, public garden—even electricity. The new communities seemed to offer the farmers many advantages, and the GVN expected warm support.[51]

Contrary to expectations, the peasants put up a stiff resistance to this forced relocation program. To the farmers who were compelled to tear down their houses and rebuild them anew in the agrovilles, to leave their gardens and fields, ancestral grounds and tombs for these desolate, barren, hot, and cramped quarters, the agrovilles were little better than concentration camps.[52] Implementation of this GVN program was riddled with abuses and this only deepened the resentment of the peasants. The villagers, whether they were going to be moved to the new centers or not, were required to provide corvee labor for the construction of the agrovilles. They had to abandon their farm work to build the agrovilles without pay and, frequently, were even forced to provide their own food for the duration of the corvee.

> They [the peasants] had to prepare the sites, without pay and often providing their own tools, which meant building access roads, digging wide surrounding canals and interior interlacing canals, and distributing the vast amount of earth thus removed so as to provide raised foundations for houses and other buildings. At the Vi Thanh site, located in what was then part of Phong Dinh province, 20,000 peasants from four neighboring districts were brought in to begin construction.[53]

If the peasants refused to move into the agrovilles, soldiers were sent to their villages to demolish or burn their houses, and destroy their fruit orchards which usually provided them with a secondary source of income.

According to the *Pentagon Papers,* the relocations "catalyzed the most widespread and dangerous anti-GVN sentiment."[54] This peasant resistance, coupled with financial and administrative difficulties, forced the government to halt the program in early 1961. However, a new policy of population relocation for purely

---

[51] *The Pentagon Papers,* Vol. I, p. 313.

[52] "The government . . . was wrong in assuming that those selected to live in the agrovilles would willingly do so. The peasant was asked or, in most cases, compelled to abandon his old homestead with its ancestral tomb, small garden, and fruit and shade trees, for a desolate plot of ground in a strange place. He had to build his new house from materials taken from his old one, and his only help from the government was the gift of about $5.50 and the offer of an agricultural loan. The loan was necessary, because the peasant had to pay for the acre and a half of land he had been allotted. Whatever he thought of having neighbors and administrative services close at hand, he did not like the long distance which he generally had to walk to his rice fields. Many people resisted entering the agrovilles or went into them with great reluctance." Scigliano, *South Vietnam: Nation Under Stress,* p. 180.

[53] Ibid., p. 179.

[54] *The Pentagon Papers,* Vol. I, p. 312.

military purposes, the Strategic Hamlet program, was initiated in February 1962.

THE FORMATION OF THE NATIONAL LIBERATION FRONT

Successive US administrations have maintained that, in clear violation of the Geneva Accords, the insurgency in the South was planned and started by Hà Nội to conquer the South by force. However, the evidence gathered by the *Pentagon Papers* and by many Vietnam scholars has shown that in fact the uprising was provoked by Diệm's heavy repression and his calculated violation of those accords. The Việt Minh were prepared to abide by the clauses of the Geneva Agreement and wanted to see the general elections of 1956 carried out because, with their wide popular support, they would have been assured of victory. Even after Diệm had repudiated the accords and proceeded to liquidate former Việt Minh cadres and persecute peasants suspected of harboring sympathy for the Việt Minh, the Democratic Republic of Vietnam (DRV) still hoped that diplomatic pressures could be brought to bear on Diệm to carry out the agreement.[55] Hà Nội only reluctantly acknowledged the necessity for armed struggle after the cadres in the South had taken matters in their own hands and started armed resistance in self-defense.[56]

Diệm's "Denunciation of the Communists" campaign and his refusal to hold the general elections convinced the cadres in the South that political action alone was inadequate to deal with the situation. However, the policy of the DRV leadership at the time was still to restrict activities to the political field, and the Southern cadres, in spite of their misgivings, went along with this injunction. As the persecution was stepped up, however, many former members of the resistance were driven by Diệm's policy to organize themselves in old Việt Minh bases for self-defense, in spite of the order to refrain from armed action. According to an official account published in the DRV in 1974:

> From the end of 1955 to 1956, as Diệm stepped up his "denounce the Communists" campaign, the hunt for patriots and former resistance members became fiercer. Finding it impossible to live and carry on the political struggle in the countryside the latter fled to former resistance bases such as the Plain of Reeds (southwest of Sài Gòn), the U Minh jungle (between Bạc Liêu and Rạch Giá provinces on the Gulf of Thailand) or Resistance zones D and C (north and northwest of Sài Gòn). Diệm sent his troops after them. Cornered, they had to organize self-defense together with the local population. In their fight for

---

[55] "The deadlines for the consultations in July 1955, and the date set for elections in July 1956, passed without international action. The DRV repeatedly tried to engage the Geneva machinery, forwarding messages to the Government of South Việt Nam in July 1955, May and June 1956, March 1958, July 1959, and July 1960, proposing consultations to negotiate "free general elections by secret ballot," and to liberalize North-South relations in general. Each time the GVN replied with disdain, or with silence. . . . The DRV appealed to the UK and the USSR as co-chairmen of the Geneva Conference to no avail. In January 1956, on DRV urging, Communist China requested another Geneva Conference to deal with the situation. But the Geneva Co-Chairmen, the USSR and the UK, responded only by extending the functions of the International Control Commission beyond its 1956 expiration date." Ibid., p. 247.

[56] See Kahin and Lewis, *The United States in Vietnam.*

survival the first units of the Liberation Army took shape, one or two companies in strength in some places and a battalion in others.[57]

In addition, a number of former Việt Minh who had returned to the cities to lead a normal life were persecuted and had to flee. Along with South Vietnamese youths drafted in the Army of the Republic of Vietnam (ARVN) who deserted and fled, these men "formed armed units and occupied some areas to organize resistance against the Diệm forces such as Lái Thiêu in Gia Định province, or the mountain region in Rạch Giá province."[58] At the end of December 1956, six hundred prisoners in Biên Hòa jail revolted and escaped after killing the guards and seizing a quantity of weapons. They made their way to Resistance zone D and the Plain of Reeds to join the armed units which had been set up there.[59]

At the end of December 1956, a "number of Southern leaders" met in an unspecified base area to assess the situation and set forth a new direction for the movement. From this important conference emerged the historic document entitled "On the Revolution in the South" (*Bàn về cách mạng miền Nam*) in which the Southern leadership continued to emphasize the priority of political struggle, but authorized military action for self-defense. According to the NLF account, the conclusion reached at this conference was that "in order to survive and expand, [each locality] should simultaneously propel political struggle strongly forward, and in a gradual manner, depending on the concrete situation in each area, organize self-defense military struggle to reinforce [the political struggle]."[60]

In this period, armed remnants of the Southern sects which Diệm was trying to crush also took refuge in the countryside to continue their fight against him.

> Part of the Bình Xuyên force comprising about two thousand armed men under the command of Lieutenant-Colonel Võ Văn Môn, Chief of Staff of the Bình Xuyên force, took to the maquis in Resistance zone D in Eastern Nam Bộ and in the Plain of Reeds.
>
> About five hundred troops of the Cao Đài force under the command of Lieutenant-Colonel Mạnh and Major Lê Hoàng, settled down in the Dương

---

[57] Tạ Xuân Linh, "How Armed Struggle Began in South Vietnam," *Vietnam Courier*, no. 22 (March 1974), p. 20. This article is a slightly abridged translation of an article titled "Vài nét về đấu tranh võ trang và lực lượng võ trang ở Nam Bộ trước cuộc đồng khởi 1959-1960" (Some Aspects of the Armed Struggle and Armed Forces in South Vietnam Prior to the Concerted Uprising of 1959-1960), written by Việt Hồng, which appeared in the journal *Nghiên Cứu Lịch Sử*, no. 155 (March and April 1974), pp. 39-55. According to *Nghiên Cứu Lịch Sử*, "Mr. Việt Hồng is a high ranking cadre in the NLF armed forces, who participated right from the start in the military struggle movement in South Việt Nam as a member of the armed forces. This article is written with the collaboration of many liberation cadres and fighters in South Việt Nam, and of Tạ Công Trinh, the journalist." Ibid., p. 55.

[58] Tạ Xuân Linh, "How Armed Struggle Began in South Vietnam," p. 20.

[59] Ibid. According to Việt Hồng, the situation in South Việt Nam in 1956 was very complex. In addition to the dissident religious sects, there were many armed bandit gangs operating in the South. He cites the band of Chín Quỳ operating in War Zone D; that of Ba Hưng in Long Nguyên; of Tư Lóng in Tây Ninh; of Ba Sớm in Biên Hòa; the gang of Liễu and Bồi operating in Lái Thiêu, Gia Định; and those such as the one under the leadership of Long and Đại in the U Minh forest which at times had up to a thousand members. "Vài nét về cuộc đấu tranh," *Nghiên Cứu Lịch Sử*, no. 155, p. 42.

[60] Ibid., p. 45.

Minh Châu resistance base, Tây Ninh province ... A force of about two thousand [Hòa Hảo] held their ground and stayed in the countryside to carry on the fight. Three hundred persons among this number, led by a son of the late Hòa Hảo Pope Huỳnh Phú Sổ, withdrew to their base in Cần Thơ to continue the resistance.[61]

Together with a group of dissident Catholics, these religious sects formed a joint command called "Cao-Thiên-Hòa-Bình General Staff" (abbreviation for Cao Đài, Catholic [Thiên Chúa Giáo], Hòa Hảo, and Bình Xuyên) at a conference held in December 1956 in the Plain of Reeds. These groups then succeeded in contacting "anti US-Diệm forces in exile in France and Cambodia" who provided them with financial support.[62] Though they had been enemies of the Việt Minh before, these sects now joined forces with them, burying their old antagonism, in the fight against a common enemy.

Many officers and troops of the religious sects later became cadres of the Liberation Army. Some of the leaders or commanders of the religious sects took part in 1960 in the founding of the South Vietnam National Front for Liberation. Lieutenant-Colonel Võ Văn Môn and Major Huỳnh Thanh Mừng of the Cao Đài sect were appointed to the Central Committee of the Front.[63]

By 1958, however, Diệm's campaign against the armed remnants of the sects succeeded in significantly reducing their forces. Four battalions of the Hòa Hảo, however, continued operating until one of them was subdued in 1962, and the others rallied to the GVN after Diệm's overthrow in 1963.[64]

Parallel to these developments in the southern regions, the situation in Central Việt Nam, especially in old Việt Minh strongholds such as Quảng Ngãi province, was evolving in the same direction. In these areas, Diệm's harsh policies were also driving former Resistance members from the plains into old Việt Minh bases in the mountains where they received the cooperation of dissident ethnic minorities.[65] The situation made it clear to them that political struggle alone was inadequate

---

[61] Tạ Xuân Linh, "How Armed Struggle Began in South Vietnam," p. 21.

[62] Ibid.

[63] Ibid.

[64] Bernard B. Fall, "Viet Cong—The Unseen Enemy in Vietnam," *New Society*, no. 134 (April 22, 1965), p. 10.

[65] In 1955, in an effort to build "a living wall" between "the lowland centers of population and the jungle and mountain redoubts of dissidents," Diệm launched a program to resettle North Vietnamese Catholic refugees and landless families from the coastal regions of Central Việt Nam in the mountain areas inhabited by the Montagnard tribesmen. *Pentagon Papers*, Vol. I, p. 255. This encroachment by the Vietnamese on their territory, plus GVN pacification efforts and forced relocation of the Montagnards in defensible communities drew a sharp response from these minorities. Revolts broke out in the Highlands—by the "Raglay tribe in the Western part of Ninh Thuận province, [and] the Bahnar tribe in Vĩnh Thạnh in the Western part of Bình Định province in early 1958, and [by] the Cor and Hre ethnic minorities in Western Quảng Ngãi in 1959." Tạ Xuân Linh, "How Armed Struggle Began in South Vietnam," p. 22. Youths from these dissident tribes were recruited by the cadres, and the two first armed units set up in Central Việt Nam in 1959 consisted mainly of disaffected tribesmen. Tạ Xuân Linh, "Armed Uprisings by Ethnic Minorities along the Trường Sơn," Part 2, *Vietnam Courier*, no. 29 (October 1974), p. 19.

under the circumstances.

> From late 1957, former resistance fighters and other patriots who had survived the white terror campaign in South Central Việt Nam (including the areas along the eastern side of the Trường Sơn [Annamite Chains]) discussed methods of struggle which would be more effective than just political struggle alone. By this time, they had received materials sent from Nam Bộ [southern region] containing the viewpoints of the leaders of the struggle in South Việt Nam as a whole. These documents indicated clearly that, because of the brutal fascist policies of the Sài Gòn regime, there was no other way out than to use people's revolutionary violence. They also pointed to the necessity to prepare for an armed uprising to wrest back power for the people...
>
> To meet the demand of the people, especially of the national minorities, that an armed struggle should be waged, and pending the decision about a new line, the leaders in South Central Việt Nam took the initiative of gradually changing the local movement into a combined political and military struggle. Quảng Ngãi and Ninh Thuận provinces were chosen as testing-grounds for this new line. In early spring 1958, on orders from Mr. Trần Nam Trung, then top leader of South Central Việt Nam and now Minister of Defense in the Provisional Revolutionary Government of the Republic of South Việt Nam, Quảng Ngãi set about preparing for an armed uprising.[66]

On March 3, 1959, a forty-five-man armed unit (called "339"), composed mostly of members of the ethnic minorities was established in Quảng Ngãi province. "It was the first armed unit to be set up in South Central Việt Nam since 1954." And in April 1959, another—consisting mainly of Raglay tribesmen—was set up in Ninh Thuận province.[67] In late 1958 and early 1959, scattered peasant revolts began to occur in the plains areas of Quảng Ngãi province. Beginning in 1959, the situation along the Trường Sơn (Annamite Chains) in Central Việt Nam became extremely tense.

> The situation in the regions along the Trường Sơn became ebullient from early 1959. However, the leading cadres in the provinces had received orders not to let the conflict spread prior to the adoption of a new line.
>
> In the summer that year, a historic resolution reached them giving them the green light for switching from political struggle alone to political struggle combined with armed self-defense and support activities. A new page had been turned in the history of the South Vietnamese revolution.[68]

In August 1959, an insurrection broke out in the district of Trà Bồng, Quảng Ngãi province, "all the 16 villages . . . the population of which numbered more than 15,000 were completely liberated."[69] The uprising then spread to the districts of Ba Tơ, Minh Long, and Sơn Hà in the province. With newly captured weapons, the province forces grew to include three companies.[70]

---

[66] Tạ Xuân Linh, "Armed Uprisings by Ethnic Minorities along the Trường Sơn," p. 19.

[67] Ibid.

[68] Ibid., p. 20.

[69] Ibid.

[70] Ibid.

By the end of 1957 and early 1958, the focus of the *Tố Cộng* campaign was switched from the Central Highlands to the Mekong Delta, causing heavy losses to the revolutionary movement there. Experienced agents from Central Việt Nam were dispatched by the Sài Gòn government to the Delta to intensify the campaign. "Định Tường province (formerly Mỹ Tho) was chosen as a pilot province in the campaign which was to spread to the surrounding areas, in particular the former resistance zones."[71] This period has been referred to as the "darkest period" for the revolution in the South. "Hundreds of thousands of cadres and people were arrested or massacred. The self-defense organizations in the countryside were broken up. The armed forces in the resistance bases had to be reduced."[72] Gradually, in self-defense guerrilla groups were organized in the villages and liquidation of government officials and police agents was stepped up, especially in 1958. The 1974 DRV account states:

> Though this was a major setback for the revolution, the revolutionaries and the people had learnt the hard way that in order to survive and wage an efficacious political struggle they could no longer limit themselves to purely defensive methods. The most urgent thing was to punish the cruel agents and tyrants, the most reactionary forces in the countryside. Step by step the self-defense organizations were restored in the form of "armed youth organizations" or militia and guerrilla groups. By 1958, the punishment of local tyrants and the destruction of the grassroot administration of the Diệm regime had become a widely-extending mass movement.[73]

A large number of village youths fled from their villages to escape GVN persecution and oppression and joined the units that were active in the Việt Minh bases. At that time, there were some armed units operating in Eastern Nam Bộ, and six companies were active in the U Minh forest in Western Nam Bộ. "By mid-1958, a battalion sized unit was founded in the Resistance Zone D. . . . At the end of the same year, the 'Command of the People's Armed Forces' in Western Nam Bộ was set up to coordinate actions with the General Staff of the religious sects." Resistance zones C and D were then extended to the mountain regions of the "three border area" (where the frontiers of Vietnam, Cambodia, and Laos meet). Many attacks were carried out in Biên Hòa, Thủ Dầu Một, and Tây Ninh province, supplying the insurgents with additional weapons which in turn permitted the formation of new units in these areas.[74]

In 1959, the *Tố Cộng* campaign reached its peak with the issuance of Law 10/59, and in July of the same year the agroville program was initiated to meet the growing threat of the insurgency. Sweep operations were launched with more urgency and frequency, inflicting heavy losses in lives and property to the peasants, thus deepening their resentment of the government. In mid-1959, the Party leadership in the South issued a new policy allowing the movement to switch from political struggle alone to armed activities combined with political action. Military activities were most intense in Eastern and Western Nam Bộ where armed

---

[71] Tạ Xuân Linh, "How Armed Struggle Began in South Vietnam," p. 22.

[72] Ibid.

[73] Ibid.

[74] Ibid., pp. 22-23.

units and bases had been set up, and peasant revolts began to occur in these areas. In Central Nam Bộ, the first "concerted uprising" *(đồng khởi)* took place in Bến Tre province in January 1960, under the leadership of Mrs. Nguyễn Thị Định.[75]

Up until that time, the DRV had been following a policy consistent with the Soviet line of "peaceful coexistence" which was implicit in Khrushchev's famous 1956 de-Stalinization speech and then announced by him in 1957. The DRV was then rebuilding its economy which had been badly damaged by the Nine Year Resistance war and encountering internal difficulties caused by its land reform program, and did not wish to see hostilities flare up again in the South.[76] From 1956 to 1959, the DRV was hoping that the situation in the South could be solved peacefully through diplomatic means.

By late 1958, the DRV was confronted with the fact that an armed insurgency was already under way in the South and had to alter its policy to take this new reality into account. In early 1959, the Fifteenth Plenum of the Central Committee was held to formulate a new policy toward the South. At that time "the Party leadership realized that the situation in the South had reached a critical stage, because the entire Party organization there was in danger of being wiped out. . . . In this desperate situation the Central Committee, meeting in January 1959, authorized the limited use of armed force in the South to preserve the Party structure and to permit the development of a political struggle movement."[77] This policy was reaffirmed at the Third Party Congress held in September 1960 which also approved the formation of a united front in the South to carry out the liberation struggle.

On February 26, 1960, a battalion from the base area in Eastern Nam Bộ, in coordination with another battalion of the religious sects, carried out the first major conventional attack on the headquarters of the GVN 32nd Regiment located near the Cambodian border in Tây Ninh province. The ARVN force consisted of about two battalions, mainly recruits still under training, supported by an armored squadron and an artillery company belonging to the 13th Division. The insurgents seized an ammunition dump and used captured trucks to cart away a large quantity of weapons. Four hundred ARVN soldiers were killed and five hundred captured.[78]

This victory had an enormous psychological impact, for it demonstrated that ARVN forces could be defeated in spite of their superiority in manpower and firepower. Shortly afterward, military commands called the "High Command of

---

[75] Ibid., pp. 23-24. See also Tạ Xuân Linh, "Bến Tre, Land of Concerted Uprisings," *Vietnam Courier*, no. 27 (August 1974), pp. 6-8.

[76] "Moreover, by 1958 economic development of the North had temporarily superseded national reunification as Hà Nội's most immediate goal. Its disposition to avoid any effort at reunification that might risk the outbreak of war was undoubtedly reinforced by its dependence upon the Soviet Union for the technological and economic assistance and machinery imports so essential to its development plans. With the Soviet Union embarked upon a policy of peaceful coexistence with the United States, Hà Nội would have jeopardized her relations with Moscow by pursuing policies in the South likely to precipitate armed conflict with Sài Gòn that might in turn lead to American involvement." Kahin and Lewis, *The United States in Vietnam*, p. 109.

[77] Gareth Porter, *A Peace Denied* (Bloomington & London: University of Indiana Press, 1975), p. 13. According to Porter, Lê Duẩn, the First Secretary of the Lao Động Party Central Committee, "later told a cadre conference that by 1959 Party branches in the South had been up to 70 or 80 percent destroyed." Ibid.

[78] Tạ Xuân Linh, "How Armed Struggle Began in South Vietnam," p. 24.

Liberation Armed Forces" were set up in Eastern, then in Central and Western Nam Bộ. The South Vietnam National Liberation Front was established in December 1960, and on February 15, 1961, at a conference held in zone D under the chairmanship of Trần Nam Trung (now Minister of Defense in the PRG), the armed units in these various zones were merged into the People's Liberation Armed Forces and put under a unified command.[79]

BẾN TRE AND THE CONCERTED UPRISING

As a Việt Minh stronghold during the Resistance, Bến Tre (now renamed Kiến Hòa by the Ngô Đình Diệm government) was subjected after 1954 to a fierce GVN drive aimed at eliminating communist influence in the province. A large network of posts and watch towers was set up to cover the 115 villages in the province. The *Tố Cộng* campaign was carried out with particular zeal in Bến Tre, and, "[a]ccording to a report of the Committee of the National Front for Liberation in Bến Tre, in the period 1954-1959", 2,519 former Việt Minh and their peasant sympathizers were killed, 17,000 others jailed or deported, and countless others were tortured.[80]

With the reestablishment of Sài Gòn control, landlords who had fled the province during the Resistance came back to their villages to reclaim the land that the Việt Minh had distributed free to the peasants. These returned absentee landlords now forced the peasants to pay retroactive rents which they had been unable to collect during the war years, and raised the rents to 40 to 50 percent of the crop yields. "According to a report of the NLF in Bến Tre, 25,600 hectares of land were thus retaken from the peasants."[81]

In 1959, as part of its population relocation program, the Diệm government set up four *khu trù mật* (agrovilles) in Thanh Thới village (Mỏ Cày district), An Hiệp (Ba Tri), Thới Thuận (Bình Đại), and An Hiệp (Châu Thành). Soldiers were sent into the villages to force the recalcitrant farmers to tear down their houses and move into the agrovilles. Then with the enactment of the 10/59 Decree, mobile special military courts were dispatched to the countryside to intimidate the peasants. Death sentences by guillotine were carried out on the spot. Persecution of former members of the Resistance was stepped up, and according to the 1974 official DRV account, "In the years 1954-1959, no fewer than 90 percent of the most loyal cadres were massacred or thrown into jails, and 85 percent of the grassroots revolutionary bases were destroyed."[82] The few remaining cadres, including Mrs. Nguyễn Thị Định herself, had to live in conditions of extreme privation and hardship in deserted, swampy areas, and to be constantly on the move to keep one step ahead of GVN agents. Yet they managed to survive and to keep the movement alive with the support of sympathetic villagers who provided them with food and shelter at tremendous costs to themselves.

Hounded by the GVN, the cadres in the province saw armed insurgency as their only means of survival and chafed under the instruction not to resort to armed action against their tormentors. Popular anger against the GVN made them realize that

---

[79] Ibid., pp. 19 and 24.
[80] Tạ Xuân Linh, "Bến Tre, Land of Concerted Uprisings," p. 4.
[81] Ibid., p. 5.
[82] Ibid., p. 6.

recourse to force would meet with an enthusiastic response from the peasants. News of armed resistance occurring in other areas of the country made the cadres even more impatient to take up arms in self-defense. In mid-1959, the Southern revolutionary leadership decided to switch from a "purely political struggle" to a combination of political and military action. This decision was communicated to the Central Nam Bộ leadership at a regional conference held in December 1959, which Mrs. Nguyễn Thị Định attended.[83] Bến Tre at that time had no armed units in operation (Việt Minh troops in the province having regrouped to the North in 1954 in compliance with the Geneva Agreements), and GVN persecution had drastically reduced the number of cadres in the province. At the conference, Mrs. Định pleaded for weapons, but there were none available. Undaunted, she decided that the province could emulate the experience of the 1945 August Revolution when the province rose up bare-handed to seize power. On January 2, 1960, she held a conference with a number of Bến Tre province cadres to discuss making preparations for the uprising. "With barely 162 cadres, 18 leading committees of the revolution in the villages and four old rifles left, she and other cadres of Bến Tre province, however, were not discouraged."[84]

The uprising was scheduled to take place from January 7 to 25, 1960 in the three districts of Minh Tân, Mỏ Cày, and Thạnh Phú, with Mỏ Cày chosen as the focal point. Preparations were completed in sixteen days, and as planned, the insurrection broke out first in Định Thủy village, Mỏ Cày district, under the direct leadership of Mrs. Định. The *đồng khởi* caught GVN authorities completely by surprise and gained momentum with the enthusiastic participation of the peasants. From Mỏ Cày the uprising spread to the other districts. Isolated posts were seized or their defendants forced to withdraw. Local GVN officials and agents were captured (those who escaped fled to the safety of the district or province towns), but only those who had harmed the people were brought out for a public trial. The most brutal among them were executed after the higher revolutionary authorities had approved the sentence. The rest were set free after being warned. The insurgents also infiltrated the Thành Thới agroville and destroyed it with the assistance of the villagers who had been relocated there. Along with the abolition of the GVN village apparatus, land belonging to the "reactionary landlords" was seized and redistributed to the poor peasants.[85] In addition, with the newly captured weapons, the first armed platoon in the province since 1954 was set up and presented to the people on January 19, 1960. This platoon later expanded to company size and, along with the guerrilla teams which were formed in the villages in the wake of the uprising, successfully repulsed a large GVN counterattack launched on January 24, 1960.[86]

Thus, without the support of armed units and practically bare-handed, the cadres and people of Bến Tre province succeeded in carrying out a momentous uprising. Because of this achievement, the fame of Bến Tre spread to the entire

---

[83] Ibid. See also Tô Minh Trung, "Ngọn cờ đầu của phong trào đồng khởi toàn miền Nam Việt-Nam" (The First Banner of the 'Concerted Uprising' Movement in all of South Vietnam), *Nghiên Cứu Lịch Sử*, no. 118 (January 1969), p. 49.

[84] Tạ Xuân Linh, "Bến Tre, Land of Concerted Uprisings," p. 6.

[85] Ibid., p. 8. See also Tô Minh Trung, "Ngọn cờ đầu của phong trào đồng khởi toàn miền Nam Việt-Nam," p. 52.

[86] Ibid., and Tạ Xuân Linh, "Ben Tre, Land of Concerted Uprisings," p. 8.

Mekong Delta, and the province became known from then on as *cái nôi đồng khởi* (the cradle of the concerted uprising). In September 1960, "learning from the experience of Bến Tre, the leading body of the revolution in South Việt Nam proper decided to launch a general uprising throughout the provinces in Central Nam Bộ."[87] Chosen as the "core for the whole region," Bến Tre launched a second wave of uprisings which spread to the entire province and lasted for twenty-two days. The second wave was even more successful than the first because the cadres had learned many lessons from their previous effort and, as the insurrection in the whole Central Nam Bộ region forced the GVN to disperse their troops, Bến Tre succeeded in destroying "sixty more posts and watch towers, liberating forty-eight more villages which formed a single stretch of land over a wide area."[88]

On December 26, 1960, six days after the foundation of the National Liberation Front for South Vietnam, the National Liberation Front Committee for Bến Tre province was presented to the population at a huge rally attended by ten thousand people.

As an offshoot of the concerted uprising movement, a new form of political struggle, called the *đấu tranh trực diện* (face-to-face struggle) was devised in Bến Tre province. It was usually carried out by a large group of women marching into the district or province towns to present petitions to GVN authorities, protesting the atrocities committed by Sài Gòn troops on an operation, the criminal activities of local officials, or demanding compensation for losses in lives and property inflicted by GVN soldiers and officials. These demonstrations and public denunciations of GVN activities were a great embarrassment to GVN provincial authorities, for they did not know how to deal with them, since the demands were legitimate. Moreover, the fact that the demonstrators were mostly women made the officials hesitant to resort to force to suppress them, for they were afraid of looking cowardly and becoming the laughingstock of the people. These face-to-face struggles proved to be a valuable political tool for the National Liberation Front. And the women who carried them out came to be known as the *đội quân tóc dài* (soldiers with long hair) and hailed for their contribution to the revolution.

---

[87] Ibid., p. 9.

[88] Ibid. According to Tạ Xuân Linh, "All told, in the course of two successive drives of concerted uprisings in 1960, the insurgent forces of Bến Tre province captured or forced the evacuation of more than one hundred posts and watch-towers, completely liberated seventy-two of its hundred-odd villages, and seized 1,700 assorted weapons. The peasants recovered more than 25,000 hectares of ricefields." Ibid., p. 9.

CONCLUSION

As has been seen above, Diệm's harsh suppressive policies and persecution antagonized the peasantry and were the root causes of the insurgency in the South. The struggle there grew out of the local social environment and was led by Southerners who had to resort to force to defend themselves. As Mrs. Nguyễn Thị Định explained in her memoir, for them there was "no other road to take," no other choice, but to follow the path of armed revolution for survival.

Mai Elliott
December 1975

No Other Road to Take
(Không Còn Đường Nào Khác)
Memoir of Mrs. Nguyễn Thị Định

Translated by Mai V. Elliott
Recorded by Trần Hương Nam

Nhà Xuất Bản Phụ Nữ
Hà Nội - 1968

PUBLISHER'S INTRODUCTION

At the meeting commemorating the twentieth anniversary of the founding of the Vietnamese Women's Union, President Hồ said, "The Deputy Commander of the Liberation Armed Forces is Miss Nguyễn Thị Định. Our country alone in the whole world has such a woman general. This is a glorious thing for the South and for our entire nation." Indeed, for a long time now the fame of Mrs. Nguyễn Thị Định, the Deputy Commander of the South Vietnam Liberation Armed Forces, has made the women in the North feel extremely proud and encouraged.

Mrs. Nguyễn Thị Định—whom we usually refer to affectionately as sister Ba Định—joined the revolution before the August Revolution. She contributed to the preparations for the successful August Revolution in Bến Tre province. And it was also there, in her native province, that she took charge of leading the women's movement and many other important tasks during the entire nine-year Resistance against the French. During the resistance against the Americans, along with the leadership committee of the province, she overcame countless difficulties, hardships, and miseries, clung with determination to the people and the land in order to mobilize the masses to advance forward toward the concerted uprising, smash the vise-like grip of the enemy, propel the revolutionary movement in Bến Tre province forward, and continuously attack the enemy with political means combined with military struggles.

She made a great contribution to the consolidation and expansion of the enormous effectiveness of the "long haired troops" (đội quân tóc dài) which sowed terror among the enemy. At the end of 1960, she was one of the founders of the National Liberation Front in Bến Tre province and was assigned to take charge of the military mission. In 1961, she was elected Chairman of the South Vietnam Liberation Women's Association, member of the Presidium of the South Vietnam National Liberation Front, and Deputy Commander of the South Vietnam Liberation Armed Forces.

In 1966, in response to the announcement of an emulation [drive] between the women of North and South issued by Mrs. Nguyễn Thị Thập, Chairman of the Vietnamese Women's Union, Mrs. Định—on behalf of the South Vietnam Liberation Women's Association—called on all women in the South to emulate the women of the North to propel forward the high tide of the women's movement struggling against the Americans to save the country.

This year, on the occasion of the fifty-eighth anniversary of International Women's Day of March 3, of the commemoration of the Trưng Sisters, and of the seventh anniversary of the founding of the South Vietnam Liberation Women's Association, while the Southern revolutionary movement is sweeping forward like a rising tide and a gushing torrent, while it is rendering the enemy prostrate, and while the people and troops of the South are rushing forward in the momentum of their victory to attack the enemy continuously and score successive victories, achieving extraordinary feats of arms which ring through the rivers and mountains, and pushing the American imperialists and their lackeys into a corner, the Women's Publishing House is reissuing the book *Không còn đường nào khác* (No Other Road to Take), the memoir of Mrs. Nguyễn Thị Định, which was published by the Giải Phóng (Liberation) Publishing House in 1966.

Because of the factor of time and because of current circumstances, the memoir *Không còn đường nào khác* only recorded a few phases of struggle in the extremely rich and exciting revolutionary career of Mrs. Định, as well as of our people and women in the South in general. However, the memoir does reflect in part the power of the people's war, the typical features of the concerted uprising movement, and the intense patriotism, the determination to fight and win victory, the resourcefulness and the indomitable and firm spirit of struggle of the people and women of the South. Mrs. Nguyễn Thị Định represents the women of the South [who are] "heroic, indomitable, loyal and resourceful." Learning from her, the women in the North enthusiastically emulate the heroic women of the South, make utmost efforts to propel forward the "three responsibilities" movement, and contribute to the great task of our entire nation which is to liberate the South, protect the socialist North, and advance toward national reunification.

We solemnly introduce *Không còn đường nào khác* to our readers.

March 8, 1968
Women's Publishing House

PART ONE

I

By the time I was ten years old, my father no longer had to work day and night rowing a sampan for hire, and my family was no longer in a situation in which my mother would have to force herself, a few days after giving birth, to sit up and sew [to earn a little extra income]. We now had enough to eat and were not as hardpressed economically as before, because we children—"the flock of ten blackbirds"—had grown strong enough to work in the ricefields, tend the vegetable garden, and catch fish. I was the youngest in the family and could not as yet perform heavy manual labor, so I usually rowed the sampan and went to sell fish with my sister-in-law. We got up at 2:00 or 3:00 A.M. every day, rowed all night, and arrived at the Mỹ Lồng market in the morning. After selling the fish, we hurriedly turned around and went home. Sometimes I made a great effort, and hoisted a heavy basket full of shrimps on my head to carry to the market to sell. The water trickled down and made my head soaking wet, but all I could manage to sell was ten cents worth of shrimps. Seeing me, many women clucked their tongues:

—My, whose daughter is that skinny girl who can row a sampan so well?

Being afflicted with asthma, I coughed and was sick often. No medical treatment did any good, so that at the age of ten I was still as thin as a stick, and not fat as I am now. My mother often said that my birth was difficult because she was already getting old and because she had given birth so many times before. Besides she had had to work very hard and had lacked an adequate diet [during her pregnancy]. When labor set in, she was in great pain for a long time. The midwife wanted to pull me out, sacrificing me to save my mother's life. My father was against it and said:

—Just leave it alone, when the time comes it will come out.

Fortunately, both my mother and I survived. This was the reason why I was the favorite in the family. My parents wanted to send me to school, but the school was located in Mỹ Lồng market, more than ten kilometers away. It would be too far for me to go there and come back every day, and if I boarded there it would be too expensive. I had to study at home, and Ba Chẩn, my older brother, taught me. He was very kind and twice my age. He was a very good fisherman and farmer, and everyone in the family loved him. He did not spare any efforts to teach me and did so with happiness and good cheer, unlike my sister Mười who was always in a foul temper, scolding, and scowling. The whole family loved to listen to Chẩn read the *Lục Vân Tiên* poem.[1]

Whenever we had nothing to do at night, we would gather around the oil lamp—my mother lying in the hammock, cradling her grandchild, my father sitting silent in front of a small tea pot, my sisters sitting around mending clothes. We all kept quiet and listened to my brother read the story fluently. As for me, although I had only learned to read printed letters, I sometimes replaced my brother and read for the whole family. People in my neighborhood also loved to listen to the *Lục Vân Tiên* story. Whenever they heard of an opera being performed somewhere, they would try to go and see it, no matter how far they had to go. Then, the next morning, as they rowed their sampans the opera addicts would repeat the new sections of *Lục Vân Tiên* they had just learned. So, in the evenings [*Lục Vân Tiên* was recited in our home], as soon as my brother or I began to read, the neighbors would all come. Sometimes, when I reached the part of the story where Nguyệt Nga, Vân Tiên, and his young valet were harmed by the wicked people, I wept and the neighbors also wept. Once in a while, my father nodded his head in approval and commented:

—This story teaches people all the virtues they must have in life: humanity, kindness, filial piety, courage, determination, and loyalty.

To show her agreement, my mother did not say anything but softly sang a few verses to lull her grandchild to sleep:

"In the Netherworld, if your soul is blessed with power,
Mother, please be aware of your son's sincere feelings.
All around me, rivers have their sources and trees their roots,
You bore me in your womb for nine months,
And my gratitude and debt to you is boundless."[2]

Gradually, in this manner, the beautiful images of Vân Tiên and Nguyệt Nga filled my mind. I hated those in the old days who abused their power, position,

---

[1]*Lục Vân Tiên,* a novel in verses, was composed by Nguyễn Đình Chiểu (1822-1888), a famous scholar of Gia Định province (South Vietnam). It is considered one of the masterpieces of Vietnamese literature. It was written in *nôm* (demotic) characters and contained two thousand verses. *Lục Vân Tiên* is the love saga between Lục Vân Tiên, a young scholar, and Nguyệt Nga, a beautiful and virtuous girl. After many misadventures and sufferings caused by wicked people, they were finally reunited. The story upheld the Confucian virtues of filial piety, loyalty, integrity, humanity, and female chastity (symbolized by Nguyệt Nga). It also contained the Buddhist doctrine of *nhân quả*: good and virtuous people will always be rewarded in the end, while the wicked will be punished. Written at a time when Vietnamese society was being put under enormous pressure by the French invasion, *Lục Vân Tiên's* reaffirmation of the old traditional moral virtues had great appeal among the people. It has remained one of the favorite literary works among the people, especially in the South, a great many of whom can recite the verses—which are written in a simple but beautiful style—by heart. *Trans.*

[2] Vân Tiên was on his way to take the literary examination when he heard the news of his mother's death. Struck with grief, he wept until he went blind. When he returned home, he went to her grave to pay his respects and express his sorrow. This scene quoted above took place at the graveside, when Vân Tiên appealed to his dead mother's spirit to come back and witness his sorrow. *Trans.*

and wealth to harm honest people like Vân Tiên and Nguyệt Nga. But I did not
know enough as yet to understand that I should also hate the wicked people who
were bringing miseries and poverty to my family and other families at the time. On
one occasion, the landlord in the village came to my house and demanded paddy in
a threatening manner. My parents had to hastily prepare food and wine to regale
him. We were out of chickens then, so they had to catch the hen about to lay eggs
which I had been raising and slaughter it for him to eat. When he finally left, his
face crimson with all the drinking, I broke down and cried in anger, and demanded
that my mother compensate me for the hen. In that period (1930) I noticed that my
brother Ba Chẩn came and went at odd hours. Sometimes men came to the house, sat
and whispered for a while, and then disappeared. One day, I heard whispers in
the room, I looked in and saw my brother hand to my father a piece of red cloth
embroidered with something yellow inside. Seeing me, he ran out and pulled me
inside, signaled to me to keep quiet and said:

—Don't breathe a word or our heads will be lopped off.

My father quietly went into the garden, climbed to the top of the coconut tree,
and hid the package there. Threatened by my brother, I hastily nodded my head
in assent, but felt very annoyed and wondered what the fuss was all about. A few
days later, as I was walking toward the market carrying the fish basket on my
head, I suddenly heard many people whisper to each other:

—There's a hammer and sickle flag at the three-way confluence of the Hương
Điểm river.

—The Communists in Bến Tre Province[3] will soon rise up like those in Phú
Riềng.[4]

All at once many things rose in my mind: hammer and sickle flag, Communism,
Phú Riềng. On the way back from the market, I went all the way to the three-way
confluence of the Hương Điểm river to take a look. I had the vague feeling that
the flag was exactly the red piece of cloth that I had seen in my house a few days
before. The yellow lines I could not make out now appeared clearly as the crossed
hammer and sickle. I did not understand anything, but felt very happy about what
my brother had done.

A few days later, my older brother Ba Chẩn was suddenly arrested by the
puppet village officials who took him and jailed him in Châu Thành district (that
is to say present day Giồng Trôm district). My mother and whole family worried
and cried a lot. This happened at the end of 1930. I often went to visit him in jail
because I was small and would not arouse the suspicion of the enemy. Every day I
had to row a sampan for more than four kilometers to bring him food. It was there
in the prison that I witnessed for the first time scenes of brutal torture. It was

---

[3] Bến Tre was the native province of Mrs. Nguyễn Thị Định. *Trans.*

[4] Phú Riềng was a large rubber plantation located in Eastern Nam Bộ (South Vietnam). On
February 4, 1930, more than one thousand workers in Phú Riềng revolted, disarmed the
soldiers, and controlled the plantation for twenty-four hours. This marked the start of the
powerful struggle movement of the proletariat under the leadership of the Indochinese
Communist Party. *Footnote in text.*

Muôn, the same Canton Chief—the tyrannical landlord who had come to my house to collect rent, drink, and swallow my hen which was about to lay eggs—who now angrily hit the prisoners with a walking stick while drinking and shouting:

—The Communists slash people's bellies and stuff rice husks in their stomachs, but [I'll go them one better] I'm going to cut open your stomachs and stuff them with one hundred piastre notes. You heard me clearly?

Then he ordered his cronies to beat the prisoners with large sticks, tie their hair, and hoist them to the ceiling by the hair. My brother was not the only one who was tortured, many other old and young people were also tortured. Many men were beaten until they passed out, blood trickling from their mouths, heads, and feet, and dyeing the cement floor a greyish and purplish color. I loved my brother and I hated the soldiers so intensely that I wanted to run out to hold them back and defend my brother, but I was too frightened so I just stood there, frozen, and wept in anger.

For many long months, I saw each day with my own eyes the arrogant and brutal soldiers beat up my brother and many other people. And it was at that moment that a thought sprang up in my innocent mind: "Why are good and capable men who are loved by the people and their families, like my brother Ba Chẩn, suddenly being beaten so savagely? Why is the gang of Canton Chief Muôn abusing their power and position to oppress poor and kind people like my brother?" Right after my brother was arrested, I asked my mother why he had been taken away. She replied:

—Because he's a subversive.

I asked:

—What does it mean to be a subversive?

My mother got angry:

—Stop it, I'm so worried and sad as it is, don't ask any more questions.

I had to shut up, but from then on I impatiently waited for my brother to return home so I could ask him to explain everything in detail. My brother was not released until half a year later. We wept with joy. He loved me even more than before because I was the only one in the family who had taken care of him during his imprisonment. I asked him:

—You didn't do anything to them, then why did they beat you up so brutally?

He smiled and said:

—Of course I did something, why not?

—You mean you were a subversive?

—Don't be silly! I make revolution to overthrow the landlords who are oppressing and exploiting us, like Canton Chief Muôn and also to overthrow the French who have stolen our country from us.

He explained to me at great length, but I did not understand anything more than that the Communists loved the poor and opposed the officials in the village. My love for my brother and the men who had been jailed blossomed and deepened with such new and significant events. When I remembered the villagers' comment that the Communists would soon rise up in Bến Tre province, I immediately thought that the time was coming when Canton Chief Muôn —the viper of two cantons in Châu Thành district—would perish. I was very happy and eagerly looked forward for that day to arrive.

It was from that time onward that I knew my brother was making revolution. I began to understand and to firmly believe that making revolution was a good thing, since my brother continued to do it even though he had been jailed and beaten up for it. I thought, "It must be very difficult to make revolution, since I'm a girl I doubt that I can do it."

In 1936, I was sixteen years old. Since I had recovered from my asthma, I grew very tall, much taller than before, and I was less skinny, though I had not put on much weight. Once in a while when I stole a look at myself in the mirror I felt very happy because my complexion was pink and healthy, and because the pallor and sallowness of the old days had vanished. Suddenly my hair became curly and wavy near the temples. My girl friends used to tease me:

—Định, did you wave your hair because you're about to get married?

I only smiled because in my head I was entertaining ideas very different from those of my friends. At that time the movement was on the rise. People from many areas frequently came to hold meetings in my house. My brother Ba Chẩn persuaded me to help and cook for them. I agreed at once. They all treated me with affection like my brother Ba. They were all good people and my parents were very fond of them. Among the men who frequently came to my house in that period were Tư Phát, disguised as a welder; Bảy Khánh and Nhựt Quang who had shaved their heads and become monks; Cò Trà, disguised as an itinerant merchant selling the ointment produced by Nguyễn An Ninh[5] in order to facilitate his propaganda work for the revolution. Trà usually wore an old and untidy jacket and a pair of pyjama pants—one leg of which was shorter than the other—but when he spoke, he was spellbinding. Once in a while, I rowed him to the market to sell his ointment. After I finished selling fish I went to where he was and saw many people still surrounding him and listening to him talk. Another person whom I was extremely fond of was Mrs. Ba Théng. She was about ten years older than I was; her husband later was deported all the way to Madagascar.[6] Mrs. Ba Théng sold imitation gold jewelry in Bến Tre and always covered herself with gold jewelry to deceive the enemy and to carry out revolutionary activities. The last person in the group was Bích, a famous intellectual in Bến Tre city. He towered over me by a head, and his face was bony and white. He was a cheerful and open person who often had

---

[5] Name of a revolutionary in that period. *Footnote in text.*

[6] A large island off the coast of Africa. *Footnote in text.*

friendly chats with my family so we all loved him. These were the people who often came to my house. There was also another group who only came once in a while and then left immediately.

At first, seeing that several of the men were living in the pagoda disguised as monks, I thought that Buddhism and revolution was the same thing. Besides, my parents were fervent Buddhists and this influenced me. I imitated my parents and fasted six days a month. Later, I stopped fasting and wanted to join the revolution, but every time I asked to be allowed to go, the people who came to my house said:

—If you want to carry out revolutionary activities you can do it at home, you don't have to leave and go anywhere to do that.

From then on, besides cooking when they came to hold meetings, I was given the job of delivering letters, propagandizing people in the hamlets and village to join mutual aid associations and rice transplanting and hoeing teams, encouraging people to buy the *Dân chúng* (People) newspaper, and mobilizing women to participate in the May 1 commemorative meeting in Bến Tre province town. Whatever task I was given I performed with a lot of zeal.

One day my brother Chấn called me into the room—the same room where he had whispered to my father and handed him a package of documents years ago. He took down a large package from the ceiling and asked me:

—Would you dare to disseminate these leaflets?

I was both happy and worried, and said:

—Alright, but unless you tell me how to do it, I won't know what to do.

He smiled and gave me detailed instructions. Finally, he reminded me:

—If the enemy catch you red-handed, just tell them over and over again that these papers were given to you by a man who said that they were publicity pamphlets for drugs. You are illiterate so you don't know what the papers say. The man told you to disseminate the papers, gave you some money, and then disappeared you don't know where.

After accepting this honorable task which was assigned to me for the first time, I felt agitated and restless. In the afternoon, I crawled inside the mosquito net and pulled out one leaflet to read in secret. Not knowing how to read very well, I had to spell each word slowly, and it took me a long time to read the leaflet. It was an appeal to the peasants to oppose the cruel rich people and village officials. That night, I could not sleep in peace and got up at midnight. At 3:00 A.M., I pretended to leave to sell fish as I had been doing every day. I gradually let the leaflets, which I had tucked under my pants at the waistline, fall down to the ground at my feet. When it was almost daylight and I was at the market, I had gotten rid of all the leaflets. The sky began to brighten. At around 8:00 A.M., the people started whispering to each other, and rumor was thick that the Communists had spread a lot of leaflets. Policemen hurriedly grabbed their weapons and ran off in a panic.

The moment I got home I boasted to my brother about the result. He congratulated me:

—You're very good. Keep on doing it and you'll become used to it.

The next time, my brother assigned me to disseminate leaflets in the Mỹ Lồng market. I also accomplished my mission. After succeeding in a few tasks, I became very eager to operate and wanted to leave because if I stayed home a lot of chores, such as cooking, working in the ricefields, and tending the vegetable garden, would get in the way of my work. I began to move around more, [going on mission]. Some nights I stayed out and came home very late. My parents were afraid I would become "bad" and said, "State affairs are not for girls to take care of. And even i f women can do it, they must be very capable. What can our daughter Định do? If she's caught, she'll confess everything and harm others." At that time, I had reached the puberty period and caught the attention of many youths in the village. Several sent matchmakers to my house to ask for my hand. My parents wanted to accept and give me away in marriage to put an end to their worries, but I absolutely refused to go along. I often confided to my brother Ba:

—I only want to work for the revolution, I don't want to get married yet.

II

It was because of my personal problem that once my sister Mười and I had a big row. She wanted to get me to marry a rich relative of her husband's. I adamantly refused to go along, and this made her angry. This unexpectedly became known to the men who came to my house to hold meetings. That afternoon, I was weeding in the garden when Tư Phát came out to lend me a hand. Tư was a cheerful person who frequently told me stories about the revolution. That day, he asked me affectionately:

—Why have you refused several offers of marriage?

I remained silent, crushing a blade of grass in my hand. A little later, I told him the truth:

—You and the other brothers must allow me to leave and join the revolution, i f I stay home my parents will give me away in marriage to someone.

He burst out laughing:

—No matter where you go you'll have to get married eventually. Do you think you can run away from it?

Seeing the weakness of my argument, I had to say:

—To tell you the truth, if I get married, I'll only do it with someone who is a revolutionary.

Phát asked me to make sure I understood what I was saying:

—If your husband is a revolutionary he'll be jailed and he'll be killed, aren't you afraid of this?

At that point someone came to fetch Tư for an urgent business. I repeated again:

—Please, you and the other brothers must find a way to let me go.

A few days later the brothers came to hold another meeting. I cooked and took care of them as usual. I was busy in the kitchen when Tư Phát came in and said:

—Bích asks you to go out and talk with him near the row of tangerine trees.

I asked him:

—What does he want to talk with me about?

Tư only smiled:

—You'll find out when you go there.

I felt thrilled and nervous. Perhaps Bích would allow me to leave and join the revolution. That afternoon, in great agitation, I went into the garden and headed straight toward the row of tangerine trees. Bích was already there, and was absorbed in admiring the dense clusters of ripe tangerines. Hearing a noise, he turned around. Suddenly I felt very awkward. He asked me calmly:

—Miss Dinh, you talked with Tư Phát the other afternoon, didn't you?

I answered in panic:

—I didn't say much of anything.

—Let me ask you truthfully, why do you want to marry a revolutionary?

I plucked a few tangerine leaves and then said:

—Because I want to leave and work for the revolution as you're all doing.

—In your opinion, what kind of man should your husband be like?

I was so embarrassed I did not know what to say, but out of respect for him [I had to come up with a] reply:

—He must permit me to work for the revolution, he must treat my parents well and love me for the rest of his life.

He looked at me attentively, and then smiled and said:

—Is that all?

At that point, I became bolder:

—Actually, I don't want to get married yet, I only want to ask you and the other brothers to allow me to leave and join the revolution.

He asked me affectionately:

—Alright, have you really made up your mind?

I was overcome with joy and nodded my head. Bích seemed lost in thought. After a while, he looked straight into my eyes and asked to test me:

—If your husband is in the revolution, he might be killed, and sometimes he might even be jailed for nine or ten years, do you think you can wait for him that long?

I lowered my eyes, my cheeks were burning with embarrassment, and then I said hesitantly:

—Yes.

That afternoon Bích asked me many questions. I answered him but did not ask him about anything. After we finished talking, I plucked a few tangerines for him to eat and then went back to the house. A thought crossed my mind: perhaps Bích wanted to . . . But I chased it away, because I thought Bích was a famous intellectual while I was just a simple country girl. Mrs. Ba Théng had told me that the daughter of the man who owned the Hàm Vàng store at the market place—a beautiful and rich girl—was running after him. However, she wanted him to become a Catholic, and he refused. After Bích left my brother Chẳn called me over and told me in private that Bích wanted to marry me, and asked me what I thought of it. When I heard the news, I was both happy and embarrassed, and my face burned as though I had had a sunstroke. But I still had my doubts and wondered whether Bích really loved me.

My parents who had always been fond of Bích agreed immediately. From then on, Bích frequently came to the house. He loved to stay in the garden, so we often went and sat for hours under the tangerine trees to confide in each other. We got married at the end of 1938. My husband's family called me Miss Ba [three], because Bích was the third child in the family. After we had become husband and wife, I once asked Bích:

—There were so many beautiful and rich girls running after you, why didn't you marry one of them, why did you marry me instead?

He answered half seriously, half in jest:

—Some of the city girls are hypocritical, unreliable, and not good. You're a country girl, but you're not inferior to anyone. You're kind and you've been influenced by the revolution. We will both work for the revolution, so what can be happier?

After spending a few days together, Bích again left to travel and operate. As for me, I continued working in the mutual aid associations and the rice transplanting teams of the women. Once in a while, the brothers brought back *Dân chúng* newspapers and gave them to us to sell within the organization. It was much later that I discovered that Bích was a member of the Bến Tre Province Party Committee and belonged to the group that operated openly under legal cover. He had been elected Chairman of the Soccer Association and the head of the Bus Transport Association. The people had confidence in him and loved him dearly. At that time, competition among the buses often resulted in brawls and knifings. Bích very patiently organized, educated, and united the people, and allocated to each bus a different departure and arrival schedule so they could operate in an orderly fashion and put an end to the chaotic practice of fighting over passengers. In addition, he frequently contributed articles to the newspapers, attacking the officials in Bến Tre and in Saigon. Many readers sent letters to his house, praising him. Once, he wrote an article saying that Mẫn, the District Chief of Ba Tri, was no better than the German shepherd of the Province Chief.[7] The District Chief was very angry but could not do anything to him. At that time Bích was busy with many things, so he only came home once every month or two, and then left immediately. The third time we saw each other he knew I was expecting. He was overjoyed. The next day, he made me go and see a doctor, and then bought all sorts of supplies for the baby—clothes and diapers—before leaving. He wanted to have a child very much, and especially a son. From then on, every time he came home he would call me:

—Hey, the mother of that fellow!

When they heard this the whole family laughed. In 1939 when my confinement period drew near, Bích came home and stayed a week with me. That was the longest time we spent together since our wedding. He took great care of me. One afternoon, we went to visit a relative, on the way back as we were nearing the house, I fell and my stomach began to hurt. Bích was in a panic and took me to a maternity clinic, and stayed there to wait. I went into the delivery room while he paced back and forth outside. The moment he heard the cry of the baby he rushed in to take a look. When the midwife told him it was a boy he was very happy and stayed around until midnight when he finally went home. But at five o'clock the next morning he was already back to take the baby and me home. The day I went home, he placed a cot next to the bed and slept there to help me watch the baby, afraid that in my exhaustion I might crush it in my sleep.

Our life was so happy and lovely when suddenly security police agents came to the house, surrounded it, and arrested Bích. The baby had been born only three days before. I could not control myself, fell on the bed, took the baby in my arms, and

---

[7] Under the French colonial administration, the post of Province Chief was held by a Frenchman. *Trans.*

wept bitterly, my tears falling drop by drop on his face. He awoke and began to cry. Bích recovered [from the shock] and told me:

—Please take good care of the baby. I'll certainly be back in a couple of days.

I abruptly got up and shouted:

—What has my husband done that you're arresting him?

—You'll know what he's done.

One of the security police agents said, his head tilted at a cocky angle. I swayed on my feet. Bích looked at me lovingly and comforted me:

—Just lie down and rest, nothing will happen to me, don't be afraid.

After they took Bích away, it seemed as though the earth and sky had suddenly turned black. I looked around the room, and looked at my baby and felt I was dying a thousand deaths. I was overcome with worry and grief, and had the feeling I would be separated from Bích forever. We had been married for one year, but had spent less than two months together. We had not even had time to choose a name for our baby when he was arrested. I remembered the time when my brother Ba Chẩn was beaten in jail, and felt full of pity and worry for my husband.

At the time that Bích was arrested, I also lost contact with the organization. The Democratic Front was entering a period of retrenchment. My brother Ba, Tư Phát, Cò Trà, Nhật Quang, and comrade Tranh, the Secretary of my village's Party Committee, were arrested one after the other. There was nothing for me to cling to, and I felt myself cut adrift both emotionally and spiritually. I wept for a long time but this did not relieve my suffering. There was nothing I could do except try to support my child and wait for my husband's return.

At that exact moment of pessimism and despair, Ba Bường came to see me. At the time I only vaguely knew that he was one of the leaders of the Party. It was only later that I found out he was in charge of the interprovince organization and that he led the uprising in Bến Tre province in 1940. That day Bường wore ragged clothes as a disguise and came to my house to buy pigs. He comforted me a great deal and gave me a bit of advice so profound and ardent that I remembered it long afterwards:

— Bích and the other brothers in jail are waiting for us to operate and bring them out, what do you think?

His voice was both stern and full of emotion. He did not utter a word of criticism to me, but I was suddenly reminded of my mission, and felt that I was being too weak. I truthfully asked him to allow me to stay in the local area to operate so I could take care of my baby. Bường again advised me in a friendly and resolute manner:

—If you operate locally you'll be uncovered immediately. Even if you stay put and don't do anything, you won't be safe. The best thing would be for you to go to another province.

If I went to another locality to operate I would have to leave my baby at home, since it would be impossible for me to take him along. This was a real dilemma for me, and I had to wrestle with my emotions for a long time. In the end, I made up my mind to leave him behind, but I asked Bường to give me a few more days [to make arrangements]. I would go to visit Bích and let him know. I promised I would leave with him on July 21, 1940.

On July 18, I took my baby with me and went to see my husband. At the prison, it took me a long time to obtain all the necessary papers, and in the end I was only allowed to see him for fifteen minutes. But at that point, to be able to see him for even one minute, for us to be able to look at each other's face, and for him to see the baby was good enough. Bường and my parents had told me to control myself and not to cry when I saw Bích, so that we would have time to talk with each other and so that I would not add to his suffering. But when I saw him standing behind the iron bars, looking out and smiling at me, my eyes suddenly became blurred, I felt dizzy and swayed on my feet. I noticed that he was emaciated, had lost a lot of weight, and looked haggard. I thought of scenes of enemy torture and felt full of pity for him. He stretched out his arms, took the baby, and kissed him for a long time. As we were passing the baby back and forth, I asked him about my leaving the baby behind and going off to operate as Bường had suggested. He loved his son very much, so he thought about it for a long time and then encouraged me:

—It's right for you to do that, I approve of it wholeheartedly.

I asked him:

—Is there anything else you want to tell me?

He looked at me with affection:

—I've been sentenced to five years of imprisonment and five years of deportation. I'm resigned to my arrest, but I feel very sorry for you and the baby. It's because of me that you two are suffering. Try to bring up the baby, go with the brothers to operate, and wait for my return. I'm very confident that you will overcome all challenges, as you told me before we got married.

Before I had time to add anything further, the guard came in to announce the end of the visit and to throw me out. I suddenly remembered and asked Bích hurriedly:

—What name shall we give to the baby?

—[Let's call him] On.

"On" was our first born. The guard shoved me outside. I did not leave at once, and kept walking back and forth in front of the prison gate with the baby in my arms, so my husband could see us a while longer.

On July 19, 1940, I returned home with the baby in my arms. Before the twenty-first arrived, the day on which Bường was coming to fetch me as had been pre-arranged, I was arrested by the security police. They took me to the prison in Bến Tre [province town] and kept me there for three weeks. They interrogated me about Bích's activities and then about my own. I kept saying that my only concern had been to raise my child and that I was totally ignorant about everything else. Finally they [said that they] would take me to a prison camp far away and forced me to send the baby home, otherwise they would take him away and give him to a Catholic orphanage. Heavens, their cruelty was beyond words! My husband was already in jail and my son was the only remaining source of comfort for me, but they wanted to cut him off from me too. I decided not to send the baby home and was determined to keep him with me, no matter what happened, so that mother and child could be together in life or in death. The men and women who were incarcerated with me did their best to make me see reason, and I had to resign myself to send word to my mother and ask her to come and fetch the baby. At that time, On was only seven months old. When I thought of our situation—my husband in jail in one place, me in exile in another, and the baby separated from both his parents—my heart broke to pieces. The day I handed the baby to my mother to take home, seeing his innocent face and his steady breathing as he lay sleeping, I bent down to kiss him but tears filled my eyes. The moment my mother turned around to leave, I broke out sobbing. My mother also wept pitifully. During those days I was full of worry and did not know how to relay the news to Bích.

A few days later, while I was missing my baby and feeling dejected—I had not eaten anything, and had become thin and pale—suddenly about ten soldiers opened the prison door and burst in. They handcuffed me and sister Cẩm Thường, a friend of mine who was jailed in the same cell. They took the two of us to a covered truck and then drove away for a long time. As we were driving along, I peered out but did not see any houses on either side of the road—nothing but the infinite green jungle. After leaving Saigon, we were on the road for one whole day before reaching our destination. When we asked, we learned that they had deported us to Bà Rá. This was one of the highest mountain peaks in South Vietnam, near the border with Cambodia. This region was infamous because of its insalubrious environment, and people used to say that those who went there never came back alive. As we got off the truck, I bumped into four bearded Frenchmen and over twenty soldiers armed with huge rattan whips madly hitting prisoners who had been stripped naked and tied together, and whose faces were bruised purple and covered with blood. Cẩm Thường and I whispered to each other: "We must prepare ourselves psychologically and mentally [for what is coming]."

This area was full of all sorts of animals—mosquitoes, jungle leeches, elephants, and tigers—and especially human beasts. Frenchmen with bushy beards and Vietnamese corporals and sergeants were even more ferocious than the tigers. They were always full of menace, as though they were about to devour us alive. During the day we performed corvee labor and fetched water. We worked hard but were still whipped and maltreated. The French policemen followed us and made passes at us; we resisted so they became resentful and found excuses to beat us up. Our bodies were always bruised and purple.

Of the four Frenchmen here, the captain was the most notorious for his cruelty. He usually carried a huge crushed rattan bulb, and every time a prisoner passed in front of him, he hit him on the head with it, leaving a swollen welt as big as a man's wrist. He also raised a very big German shepherd; every time he beat up a prisoner he shooed the dog to bite and tear him up so that the prisoner started to bleed all over. One time, I was weeding when this fellow who was standing on the balcony and carrying a pistol in his hand called to me and told me to hold up a bottle for him to shoot at. I refused, but he threatened to shoot me, so I had to comply. He shot the bottle to pieces and then doubled up with laughter. From then on, every time he saw me, he loaded his pistol and threatened to shoot. He said:

—This young communist female is very tough!

In that period, the movement on the outside was being savagely suppressed. Each week, they brought a few more women to the prison camp, including sisters Hai Sóc, Bé, Thước from An Giang province, Lưu, Tiếu, Nguyễn, Uông, Ba Théng, etc. Our numbers grew larger and larger. We united our forces and intensified the struggle within the camp, so that the camp authorities did not dare to terrorize us at will. I still remember the physical appearance of the corporal in the camp. His face was black, he had protruding eyes, and he always smelled of liquor. He was extremely cruel and beat up political as well as criminal prisoners. Many times we tried to educate him, but did not get anywhere. Once I told him to his face: "If you behave in such a cruel fashion, you'll give birth to children with physical defects."[8] His eyes became dilated with anger and he said arrogantly:

—If they're defective, I'll fix them with my own hands! These prisoners, if I don't beat them up like that, there'll be no discipline. If I was in charge of you women, I'd beat you even more!

—Yeah, we dare you to beat us up!

Our women's cell talked things over with the criminal prisoners and suggested that they kill the corporal to set the example for the others. Half a month later, the brothers finally found the favorable opportunity. One day, the corporal took six prisoners to dig a grave and bury a dead man. After they finished digging, the prisoners asked him to go down into the hole to check. He did. The prisoners beat him to death with shovels and picks, and then buried him on the spot. Then they all escaped from the camp. This frightened the brutes in Bà Rá and they became less vicious.

During those days of misery in the Bà Rá prison camp, the images of Bích and my son were constantly in my mind. Every time I made something, I made it for the three of us: I embroidered three pillow cases, made three pairs of chopsticks and sewed three handkerchiefs. I was still full of hope that I would be allowed to go home. Sisters Bé from An Giang province, Thước, Uông—the wife of Tư Lần; Nguyễn—the wife of Nguyễn, etc. were in the same situation as I was, their

---

[8] It is a popular Vietnamese belief that heavens will punish the wicked by visiting calamities upon their families or themselves. *Trans.*

husbands having also been deported to Poulo Condore island, so we often encouraged each other:

—In the future, when we get out, we'll all have a second wedding with our husbands, and then we'll continue to work for the revolution. Wouldn't it be wonderful?

III

My life as a prisoner in the Bà Rá mountain dragged on for three long years. At the end of 1943, I suffered from serious cardiac disorders and the enemy took me back to my native area where I was put under house arrest. Stepping out of the prison, I nurtured a lot of hope about meeting my husband and son, and brothers Bường and Tư Phát. I entered the house with great joy and happiness. My mother and the whole family ran out and embraced me with happiness mingled with sorrow. My son did not know I was his mother, so he just sat and stared. I called his name and ran over to hold him tight in my arms as though I did not want to ever let go of him. On was then four years old, and the older he got the more he looked like the exact replica of his father. This fact made me most happy. As for Bích, there had not been any news from him for two years.

Three months later, while the wounds inflicted on my body in the imperialist prison camp had not yet healed, I was dealt another staggering blow—the most painful in my whole life. Bích had died in Poulo Condore. Heavens, calamities kept coming on the heels of one another so that I no longer had enough tears left to weep away my sorrow. For a whole month afterward, I was half crazed and would laugh or get angry for no reason. Sometimes at night I groped my way out to the corner of the garden where I had met Bích for the first time, and sat down and wept. The most unbearable pain for me was that I could not tell my son about his father's death because he was still small. So I just let the pain torment me in secret. Once, On woke up in the middle of the night and suddenly asked me:

—Ma, you told me my father is in Poulo Condore, why is it that he hasn't come back?

—He's still out there, my son.

—Why is he staying there so long? When will he come back?

After he finished his questions, he went back to sleep. But I stayed wide awake and could not go back to sleep. I felt so miserable that sometimes I had the crazy idea of becoming a Buddhist nun or of killing myself. But when I looked at my son, when I thought of my husband's death, when I remembered the brothers and sisters [in the revolution], when I recalled the days of sufferings and hardships in the prison camp, I felt my resolve return and I told myself: "I must live to bring up my son and to avenge my husband and comrades." For this reason, I became even more attached to the revolution. While waiting to reestablish contact [with the revolution] I sewed for a living.

The life of a young widow like me in the old society was full of difficulties. Seeing that I was still young—only twenty-three years old—the village officials and soldiers came to my house to make advances. The village chief—that miserable old goat—sent an intermediary to persuade me to become his concubine. His wife kept coming to see me, smiling and cajoling me in the most brazen manner. Finally I had to tell her to her face:

—I know you're not doing this out of choice. Go home and tell your husband that even if the god in heaven asked me to marry him, I would refuse, not to mention a character like your husband.

The village chief resented this and made threats, but I was not scared.

In those years, the pro-Japanese movement was very active in the countryside, trying to recruit people into their organization. The pro-Japanese people came to gauge my attitude and to persuade me [to join their movement]. Even though I had not succeeded in reestablishing contact [with the revolution] and did not know what the standpoint and policy of the revolution at that juncture was, I resolutely repeated to the villagers the things that Bích and the other brothers had told me before:

—The Japanese are cruel fascists. If they rule us, five families will have to share one single knife.[9] Don't listen to their lies and deceptions.

It was only in 1944 when the Việt Minh movement became strong that I succeeded in establishing contact with the organization. Brother Hai Nhứt showed me the Việt Minh Front's Declaration, gave me guidance, and then assigned me to mobilize and organize the women in Châu Thành district. I again left my son at home and passionately plunged into my new tasks. During the tumultuous uprising [in August 1945] to seize Bến Tre province town, I was designated to carry the flag and lead thousands of people armed with knives, sticks, flags, bright red banners and placards, pouring into the province town. The mass of people marched at a brisk pace for tens of kilometers without stopping to rest, but felt neither tired nor hungry. After the successful uprising in Bến Tre province, brothers Phan Triêm, Hai Nhứt, Năm Trà, and sister Ngọc kept me and did not allow me to return to my local area and assigned me to take care of women's affairs in the province. A few days later, news arrived that Poulo Condore prisoners had been liberated. Bến Tre province received the order to welcome the political prisoners on their return from the island. Though Bích had been dead for a long time, my heart was filled with excitement for I still nurtured the hope that he was still alive.

My mother said:

—If your husband is still alive and comes back, I'll give you a pig to slaughter and celebrate.

---

[9] The implication here is that the Japanese rule would be harsh and restrictive, and, that out of fear of an armed uprising, they would not allow each family to own a knife since the knives could be turned into weapons against them. *Trans.*

I took On with me to go and welcome the brothers. On this trip, I met many brothers I knew such as Mười An and Bảy Khánh, the latter had been arrested and deported to Poulo Condore at the same time as Bích. When they recognized me, they surrounded me and asked how I was doing. They each patted On's head and said:

—He looks exactly like Bích. If you put him in a group of children, you'll still be able to pick him out.

Bảy Khánh told me with great affection:

—By continuing to work for the revolution and making progress, you're acting exactly in accordance with Bích's aspirations. If you love him, you must fight to avenge him.

Another added:

—From this moment on, you'll have to work twice as hard to make up for Bích's contribution as well, do you agree?

In the general happiness, I forced a smile and said:

—Yes.

I felt close to tears, but at the same time my heart was filled with happiness because I had done exactly what Bích had told me when I went to see him in jail with On in my arms. Now I also found out that during the entire time he was in Poulo Condore, until his death, he had always expected me to do just that.

PART TWO

IV

After the uprising, the Bến Tre Province Party Committee assigned me to operate in the Province Women's National Salvation Association. Because I had gained some experience working at the basic levels, I was assigned to go to the districts and villages to build up the women's organization network. With great enthusiasm, I left immediately for Châu Thành district and then went to Mỏ Cày and other districts. Accompanying me at this time was Lê Đoan, a student newly graduated from high school who is now a member of the Central Committee of the Vietnamese Women's Union.

At the end of 1945 and the beginning of 1946, at the Bến Tre province-wide Women's Congress, I was elected to the Executive Committee of the Women's Association. As the conference reached its conclusion, Tết [the Lunar New Year] was approaching. The Women's Association Executive Committee assigned me to organize a delegation of mothers and sisters, and a number of young girls, to go to the front to present Tết wishes to the troops.

We went to visit a unit newly returned from combat. Every one of them was covered with dust from head to foot, their clothes had been ripped by tree branches, and their hair was unkempt because they did not have anything with which to cut their hair [at the front]. We felt very moved and all shared the same profound realization, "Our troops endured the worst hardships." In spite of all the privations, they remained cheerful, laughed, and sang. We were infected by this contagious happiness and quickly became integrated with the life of the troops. Though the time we spent with them was brief, we felt a great deal of sympathy, love, and respect for them. We had actually come only to visit, present Tết gifts, and then leave, but all of us volunteered to stay longer to mend and wash clothes for the sick fighters. We stayed an extra three days. When we left, the comrades in the unit told us over and over again:

—Please report to the higher levels that we can endure any privations. But we badly need weapons and ammunition, and we hope that the higher levels would solve this problem for us. Each squad only has two or three rifles, and this makes it very difficult to fight.

I was still visiting with the troops when I was summoned back by the Province Party Committee and given a new and very special mission which I had never expected. I was chosen to be a member of a delegation going to the North to report to President Hồ and the Government, and to ask for weapons to supply the South. The delegation included Ca Văn Thỉnh and Doctor Trần Hữu Nghiệp.[10] When I heard the news I was torn between wanting to go and wanting to stay. I wanted to go and see the North, and especially to meet Uncle Hồ. The people of the South had always been jealous of the people in the North because they had the honor of living near Uncle. But I did not want to go because I felt I was still inexperienced. How would I report when I reached the North, what could I say? However, my desire to go was much stronger than my desire to stay, so when the Province Party Committee reconfirmed it, I accepted with alacrity.

Our delegation took the sea route from Bến Tre to Phú Yên province at the end of March 1946. Navigating on the undulating sea for the first time, many people became seasick and heaved until they vomited even their bile liquid. They were so exhausted they sprawled all over the boat. The most seriously ill was Doctor Nghiệp. Only brother Tư Thỉnh and I felt alright because we ate little and did not lie down. From Phú Yên, we took the train all the way to Hà Nội. Getting off in Hà Nội, I felt thrilled and excited. I was a peasant girl and during my tenty-six years had never set foot outside Bến Tre province. Now, thanks to the revolution, I had the chance to visit the capital of our country. I felt lost in every way, but one thing which immediately made me feel at home was the warm feeling and familial love of the people in the North, and this made me extremely happy.

While we were resting the news suddenly arrived that I had been summoned to meet Uncle Hồ. So, my most ardent aspiration was about to be satisfied! During the days our delegation was on the road we had discussed and prepared in advance what we would report to Uncle, what proposals we would present. As for me, I had prepared in my mind all the particular conditions of the women's movement in the South in order to report them to Uncle.

That day, we met Uncle at the Résidence Supérieure. We had just climbed up all the steps when an old man quickly stepped out and I almost shouted. That was Uncle, no mistake about it! He looked exactly like he did in his pictures. I stood frozen, staring avidly at him. He warmly shook the hand of each person. Before meeting Uncle I had thought he was a very stern man. But when we stood next to him all our worries vanished. The more time we spent with him, the more deeply I was moved by his immense love, the love of an old father for his children. That year, his hair was beginning to turn white. As I watched him talk, I noticed that he had lost one of his front teeth. The moment he sat down, he immediately asked about the situation in the South. He pointed at me:

—Women have the priority to speak first. Tell me about the situation of our people and our troops in the South. What do they lack at this moment? What do you, brothers and sisters, want to propose?

I nervously stood up. All the things I had prepared in advance to say when I saw Uncle vanished. He smiled and then asked me:

---

[10] Professor Ca Văn Thỉnh became DRV Consul General in Indonesia in 1959, and then DRV representative in Cambodia in the early 1960s. Dr. Trần Hữu Nghiệp became Director of the Training School for Health Cadres in Hà Nội after 1954. *Trans.*

—You need weapons badly, don't you? How many weapons do you, young brothers and sisters, want to take back with you?

It was miraculous! He had mentioned exactly the most crucial thing that the leading comrades in the South had told us over and over again before we left. I was overjoyed and reported to him:

—Yes, Uncle, we lack weapons badly.

He said slowly:

—The Central Committee and the Government will certainly procure the weapons to send to the South. However, our country is poor, when you young brothers and sisters go back you must fight the French well and seize their weapons to use. Then you'll have a large reserve of weapons to draw from.

During the meal, Uncle talked with each member of the delegation. He urged me:

—Stay out here for a while to attend a training class and then go back to continue the resistance with the people.

I still remember clearly—as though the words were engraved in my mind—Uncle's instructions that day:

—A revolutionary has to study all his life. He has to study theories; he has to study from the people; and he has to study from real situations. A revolutionary who doesn't study is like a man moving in the night without a light, without a walking stick, and he'll fall easily. Do you agree?

—Yes!

A few days later, the delegation of cadres from the South again had the opportunity to come and present their wishes to President Hồ on the occasion of his birthday on May 19th, 1946. He looked at us affectionately and then said:

—I have no delicacies to offer you today because our people in the South are enduring countless sufferings caused by the French. You, my nephews and my niece, and I cannot celebrate and be merry. So, young brothers and sister, go back to the South and report to our beloved people there: Old Mr. Hồ's heart and the hearts of the people in the North are always near our kindred compatriots in the South. Our whole country is united in the determination to drive out the French aggressors. We will certainly win, and North and South will be reunited as one family. When this happens, our whole country will celebrate victory together.

Then he wept, and we all wept also.

From then on, I constantly pictured in my mind the largest rally [in the history of] Sài Gòn to welcome Uncle Hồ to the South when the resistance achieved victory.

That day would be the happiest day for the people in the South, sharing in the common joy of victory of the whole country.

V

After a period of working and studying in the capital, I was very happy to return to the South. [As I was not joined by] the other members of the delegation who either stayed behind to work permanently in the North or were going to return later. I went directly to Quảng Ngãi province which was then serving as the headquarters of the South Vietnam Resistance Committee, to take delivery of the weapons, money, and documents set aside by the Central Committee [for the South], and bring then back to the South Vietnam Region Party Committee.

When I arrived, the brothers had already received the cable from the Central Committee and had prepared in advance a quantity of arms for each of the 7th, 8th, and 9th Zones of South Vietnam. The day I went to take delivery of the weapons was truly a happy and moving day. The brothers allowed me to enter the depot to take delivery of the arms reserved for the 8th Zone. All the available weapons had been equally divided among the three zones, but I pleaded and obtained the surplus weapons [for the 8th Zone]. I constantly thought of the brothers in the South waiting for me to bring back arms supplies. This was why I accepted everything the brothers [in Quảng Ngãi province] gave me and even pleaded for more. I told them:

—If I'm caught transporting just one rifle back, I'll be killed. So give me one thousand rifles to take back to make my trip worthwhile.

The comrade in charge of distributing weapons was a native of the South so he was very sympathetic:

—I'm only afraid you won't be able to carry so many weapons back!

In Quảng Ngãi the arms were put aboard a train which then took me and the supplies over a short distance to Tuy Hòa. From here southward was the enemy's zone of occupation where control was extremely tight. The only feasible way to transport these tons of weapons south was by sea, however, this route was also under tight enemy control. Every day ships and airplanes constantly patrolled the sea, and had sunk innumerable fishing boats belonging to the people. I was very concerned and tried to find a way to take this quantity of arms to the 8th Zone. To have determination was not enough and it would not be easy for me to reach my destination safely.

The brothers bought me a large old boat, the prow of which was not very pointed, capable of carrying twelve tons of cargo. I was concerned that not all the supplies would fit into the boat, and it would be a great shame if any weapons had to be left behind. To disguise the cargo and deceive the enemy, we also bought one hundred fishing nets, each costing one hundred piastres, and a large quantity of fish sauce jars which we arranged all over the deck. Late at night we quickly moved the arms supplies and stacked them in the hold. During the day we spread the nets out to dry and rearranged the jars of fish sauce, moving them around from one place to another, so as to look busy and deceive the people around us. It took us almost a week to move all the weapons into the hold of the boat. The large weapons consisted of a few submachine guns, while the rest of the hold was filled with Thomson and Mas rifles.

All the supplies had been stacked in the hold, but we still had not found any crew members to man the boat. Since this was the first and unexpected sea transport venture, [the resistance] had not arranged to have all the required personnel on hand. There were only four people making the journey: Phong, a radio operator sent by the Central Committee to reinforce the 8th Zone; two *Vệ Quốc Đoàn* (National Guards) from Quảng Ngãi province to protect the boat; and myself. Among the group, Phong had never traveled by sea; both *Vệ Quốc Đoàn* comrades were very young new recruits full of enthusiasm but lacking in combat experience. We looked for a long time and finally found four men native of Gò Công province [South Vietnam]: two men, each about fifty years old, and two youths. They had sailed their sampan all the way out here to sell rice, but unfortunately their boat was sunk by [French] airplanes, and now they were trying to find a way to return South. We studied them carefully and knew they were good participants in the national resistance movement and experienced seafarers, so we hired them to take the boat to Bến Tre province and paid them each one thousand piastres in wages.

Our cargo was ready and we had people to take us, but the boat had to remain in port because we had to wait for the wind from the northeast to rise. It was already the month of October 1946. I was impatient and felt very restless. The brothers in the [Phú Yên] Province Party Committee teased me:

—Perhaps it would be faster to unload the cargo and transport it by land!

The brothers also bought me a small round dinghy (*thuyền thúng*) costing five hundred piastres, which could carry five people without sinking, a Colt pistol, and a leather briefcase to carry the cash and documents. If anything happened we could grab the briefcase containing the pouch of money and documents and jump into the dinghy. While waiting to leave, I profited of the time available to practice rowing the dinghy and handling the pistol.

At that time, we fervently examined the sky and earth day and night, wishing that the wind would start to blow. Five times in all we prepared drinking water, bought fresh vegetables, dried fish, and got ready to set sail. But there was not a breath of wind, so we ate all our supplies, and then made preparations all over again. We spent a month waiting in vain. Once in a while, we heard the news that the French had sent ships and airplanes out to strafe fishing, boats in the open seas, killing hundreds of people each time. But we did not rose our resolve.

One evening in November 1946, suddenly the wind started to blow hard from the northeast, the sky blackened, and the sea became extremely rough and turbulent. My heart beat madly when I imagined the arrival of our boat in Bến Tre province, and forgot completely about the impending dangers. Our boat weighed anchor and surged out to sea. Later on, the brothers in the Phú Yên Province Party Committee told us that a number of people came to report to them in great excitement:

—The sea is so turbulent, why is that boat going out? Whose boat is it? Does it belong to the enemy or to us?

We learned a very precious experience during the Resistance: it was easier for us to deal with natural dangers than to cope with the dangers created by the enemy. The safest moment for us to travel was to go during a storm! When the boat was parallel to Nha Trang the wind became even more powerful. The boat was tossed back and forth. The huge waves looming on the black sea surface looked like giant monsters slithering and lunging forward as though about to swallow the tiny boat of the Resistance. I had gleaned some experience from the previous trip so I ate little that evening, bound my belly tightly, and, although I felt nauseated, I absolutely refused to lie down. Both comrades in charge of protecting the boat were vomiting till they began to throw up green bile liquid. The old men who had had a lot of seagoing experience suggested:

—Let us lower the sail, otherwise the wind would rock the boat back and forth, and it would capsize immediately.

The brothers wrestled for a long time but only managed to lower two of the sails. The boat moved very slowly. Each time it was hit by a wave, the boat seemed on the verge of being dashed to pieces. The old man who was steering the boat was small but had enormous skill. He was drenched by water but still maintained a firm grip on the helm. The two young crew members were bailing out water without stopping. I sat inside the hold but was drenched by the waves and tossed back and forth between the crates of ammunition, and my whole body ached with pain. During the night our boat remained in the open seas, not daring to move near the coastline, out of fear that we would be seen by the enemy patrol boats running along the coast.

After a tumultuous night, the wind died down, the sea became more calm, and we again hoisted our sails and the boat surged ahead. In the morning of the third day, our boat was moving parallel to Phan Thiết when we saw bobbing in the distance a French boat. Heavens, we had just escaped a natural enemy only to run into a human one! The boat crew panicked. I was slightly trembling inside, but I recovered myself and said loudly:

—Don't panic or they will find out! Just remain calm and act as we've planned.

While making preparations for the trip we had anticipated that we would certainly run into situations where we would have to fight it out with the enemy, so we had deployed two submachine guns at the ready and placed two mines at both ends of the boat. Before we left, the collectivity had met and decided:

—We must at all costs transport this quantity of arms from the Government and Uncle to the South. Even if we have to sacrifice our lives, we won't let the weapons fall into the hands of the enemy.

That was also our ironclad oath in the face of this difficult but extremely glorious task. The rice merchants knew that it was a dangerous mission, but they were good people and said unanimously:

—We have confidence in you, brothers and sister, we'll do whatever you say.

Now, a difficult challenge lay ahead of us. The enemy ship continued to advance threateningly toward us. I gave the order:

—Phong, you'll take care of the mines. Comrades Chiến and Thắng, man the submachine guns. Only discharge the mines and fire the guns when I give the order. For the moment, let's all go inside the hold.

The sky became light. The enemy ship approached, as large as a three-storied building. Soldiers armed with rifles stood all over the ship deck, looking attentively toward us. I brought out a basket full of rice, sat down, and proceeded calmly to pick out the chaff. Two of the crew members spread the nets out to dry. Outwardly I seemed very calm, but inside I felt very nervous thinking of the decisive moment which was drawing close. Many questions crowded in my head: "How should I handle their questions? If they demand to board and search the boat should we open fire and [explode the mines] to sink the boat?" As I was pondering these questions, I also prayed to the brothers, who had died in Poulo Condore, to protect the boat and help take it to the South so that the troops would have the weapons with which to avenge their deaths. I was not superstitious, but at that moment I followed without hesitation a common custom and prayed to the Genie Bổn[11] imploring that if he protected us and saw us through this danger safely, I would offer him a pig in worship when I got home. The enemy ship slid forward. The end was near! But suddenly, it turned around and moved away. It had been a close shave! After the ship had moved far away, the two young fighters in charge of protecting the boat became emboldened and cursed after them:

—Blind idiots, your ancestors be damned!

We could not suppress our laughter. But from that time on, I spent each day inspecting the sea with a pair of binoculars, afraid that if we were not vigilant we would run into the enemy again. If we had to fight, how would I direct the battle? The sails were full and the boat continued to move fast, but I felt as though it was remaining stationary. I was still worried and agitated. We had survived three days and four nights. If we had not strayed from our course, we would reach destination after five days and five nights at sea. On the fourth night, we saw a lighthouse beacon far away in the distance. The old man navigating the boat shouted happily:

—We've reached Cap Saint Jacques, brothers and sister. One more day and night and we'll be in Bến Tre.

The next day, our last day at sea, seemed very long. We all looked forward to reaching destination and bringing our boat into port. In the evening, the boat moved slowly toward the coastline. But that night we ran into a new calamity. While searching for an entry channel the boat ran aground on a sandy bar and would not budge. It was carrying tons of cargo, who would be strong enough to push it free? We

---

[11] According to popular imagination, this is a powerful spirit who usually helps human beings. *Footnote in text.*

looked toward land, but the night was dark and the darkness was vast and impenetrable, and we could not tell where we were or make out anything. The sea was immense. I asked the helmsman in which direction lay the shoreline. He signed heavily:

—I don't know anymore!

I broke out in a sweat and thought: "Now that we're here, it's dangerous for us not to know which way to go to reach the shore. The enemy's all around us. What shall we do?" The helmsman checked the water level and then exclaimed:

—The water level keeps getting lower and lower, we're doomed!

Phong was a Party member, so I consulted him first:

—If we wait for the water level to rise, who knows how long this will take. If we stay here till morning and run into the enemy, we will be like meat being offered to a cat. When the boat can float free, we won't know which way to go to enter a safe harbor, so let me go inland and find a liaison agent.

Phong was very worried and said:

—We don't know where we are, so how can you go inland? Suppose you bump into the enemy?

I thought it over for a while and then said:

—Shall we just sit here and wait for death to come? I feel I must go and find a way to save ourselves.

In the end, comrade Phong and the other brothers agreed to let me go ashore. I handed the briefcase containing the money and documents to Phong and left with Châu, a very kind-hearted boat crew member. I told the brothers that if everything went smoothly after we reached land, we would wave a torch around midnight as a signal that everything was all right. If they did not see any signal, they should withdraw and get ready to fight to protect the boat and supplies.

As the sky darkened, the two of us went down into the dinghy and rowed for a long time. I was a little worried about my risky action, but hoped that we would find the people and be rescued. We did not reach the shore until after 8:00 P.M. Though we were standing on dry land, I still felt seasick, my ears hummed, and I was unsteady on my feet as though the earth was rocking and heaving beneath me. I had to stand still for a long time to recover my senses and then felt less dizzy. In the pale moonlight, the two of us silently headed straight toward the faintly green row of trees. When we got there, it turned out to be a marsh filled with scrub trees. We were up to our knees in water and did not know which way would be the best direction to take. I was still undecided when Châu suddenly cried out:

—Sister, I see lights ahead!

I was overjoyed and quickly told him:

—Don't talk so loud!

We walked on, oblivious to everything. When we saw faint shadows of houses, I did not know whether we were in a friendly or hostile area. I stopped to check and prayed inwardly: "If anything happens, please allow me to go back to Bến Tre so that at least the brothers will know I'm back." Châu crawled forward to take a careful look and then turning around said:

—This must be a hamlet. I don't see any military post, sentries, or alert drums.

We edged closer. Seeing the lights still on in many houses and hearing people talk and even children singing, I guessed we were in a friendly hamlet. I shouted loudly:

—Friends, we've had an accident at sea, please come out and rescue us.

[We heard] thudding footsteps of people running in the settlement. Five or six youths carrying sharpened sticks ran out: "Who goes, raise your arms!" We obeyed the order. Only two of the youths approached us. I asked right away:

—Brothers, where are we?

They did not reply and shouted again:

—Keep your hands above your heads and come over here.

I walked in front, Châu followed behind in case something unexpected happened. The youths looked at me threateningly. The others remained at a distance. I repeated:

—I'm a seafarer who's had an accident, where am I, brothers?

—They remained silent and eyed me suspiciously. One youth who stood in the back and seemed to be the leader ordered the others to take us inside a house. Once inside, they separated Châu and me in order to interrogate us. A youth asked me:

—Where do you come from? Do you have any papers?

I was not completely sure which side he belonged to, so I did not dare to pose the question directly, and simply asked an indirect question:

—Is this a French or a Việt Minh area, brother?

They did not answer and kept asking me one question after another. I maintained I was simply a merchant and was on my way to Thạnh Phong to buy goods and to visit sick relatives. After questioning me over and over again for a long time, they went into another house to talk things over. I pretended to weep. The women looked at me, half trusting, half suspicious. I tried to win the sympathy of some of the older women:

—I'm an honest person, let me ask you frankly, are these men Việt Minh?

Seeing my sincere attitude, they nodded their heads and seemed to trust me:

—Yeah, something like that . . .

About half an hour later, the men returned, asked whether I could write, and told me to make out a report. I pretended I was illiterate. A youth sat down in front of me and started to write the report. I continued to pretend weeping, but at the same time I stole a look to see what he was scribbling. The youth pulled out a fountain pen and wrote clumsily on the top line: "The Democratic Republic of Vietnam, Independence, Freedom, and Happiness." I almost shouted with joy. I was about to spill out everything, but checked myself. I asked the cadre in charge to go out into the yard with me. I pulled out my letter of introduction which I had hidden in my hair and showed it to him. After he finished reading, he jumped up and down with joy:

—Heavens, this is sister Ba Định, brothers! We got the order to wait for you here a week ago, but the weather was stormy and we thought you couldn't make it.

Suspicion suddenly gave way to trust. The comrades invited me inside the house, surrounded me, and asked me all sorts of questions about our sea journey. The women immediately started to cook rice soup with duck broth. Châu went out and waved the torch three times to signal the boat. The next day, at dawn, our "ocean-going vessel" crossed the Thạnh Phong harbor safely without running into the enemy and then headed straight toward the Rạch Heo arroyo where the Thạnh Phú District Party Committee Headquarters was located. The storm had passed and our mission had been accomplished. I handed the weapons directly to Trần Văn Trà[12] who was them commanding the 8th Zone. He had come all the way down to the forest in Thạnh Phú to take delivery of the extremely precious capital that Uncle and the Government had sent to the South, and which I had had the honor of transporting here all the way from the North. All this made the troops and people in the South even more enthusiastic and determined to win victories in order to repay the enormous debt they owed the Party, Uncle, the Government, and the people of the whole country who had taken care of their kindred compatriots in the South with such utter devotion.

VI

After I returned from the North I continued to operate in Bến Tre province as I had done before. In the years 1950, 1951, and 1952, the French colonialists poured

---

[12] General Trần Văn Trà directed the Tết Offensive of 1968 and became Chairman of the Military Administrative Committee, which administered Sài Gòn after the Sài Gòn government surrendered in April 1975. *Trans.*

out all their energies to expand their oil spot to cover all of South Vietnam. Looking at the map, the blue patch denoting enemy control covered almost all of Bến Tre province. On the islets, enemy posts, big and small, appeared everywhere like a spider's web. The Province Party Committee Headquarters had to retreat toward the swampy forest at the edge of Thạnh Phú near the sea, which was the only base we had left. However, on several occasions enemy pressure and mop up operations were so fierce that we lost our foothold in Bến Tre and had to cross over into Trà Vinh to set up camp. This was the most dangerous and the most difficult period for Bến Tre during the nine years of resistance. On some days, we did not even have enough rice gruel to go around. Sometimes we had to shed blood to obtain drinking water. The enemy had set up outposts in every inhabited settlement and filled in all the wells near where they were stationed. We camped in swampy areas filled with salt water, and there was not one spot where we could dig a well, so when the situation became really critical we had to organize attacks on the posts to obtain water.

The Province Party Committee responded quickly with three policies: increase production, resolutely attack the enemy, and consolidate the base area. Besides performing our revolutionary tasks, each of us had to till one *công* of land. Land suitable for rice cultivation was not available so we had to clear [patches of] the forest and transform them into arable land. The members of the Province Party Committee Headquarters fished and grew rice for food supplies. Comrade Quang, the Secretary of the Province Party Committee, was chronically ill, and his eyes had sunk deep in their sockets, but each night he went fishing with the other brothers and then spent the day doing revolutionary work and holding meeting.

In this period I was assigned to the Liên Việt Front to operate. I stayed with the organ of the Province Liên Việt Front along with Hai Tri, my second husband who was also a Liên Việt Front cadre. My son, On, continued to live with my mother in Lương Hòa village, which was under enemy control. It was very rare that I got letters from him or received news about him. Leaving him in an area under enemy control, I was very worried that he would absorb the bad influence of the enemy, but conditions did not as yet permit me to bring him out.

Every day, the two of us, husband and wife, performed our revolutionary tasks and production work, farming our share of rice field. Hai Tri was an efficient worker and was very good at clearing forest land. While I transplanted rice, he tied the rice seedlings into bundles. Whenever they ran into us, the other comrades would tease us:

—If you have two buffaloes you'd become middle peasants!

Our life was hard but happy. When Tết came, I rowed the sampan and ferried the brothers out to catch fish, just like I used to do when I was small: rowing the sampan in the Ba Giồng river at night to sell shrimps [at the market place]. Ten years had passed, but I had not lost my skill at rowing sampans. I always felt terribly sleepy as the night advanced. Sometimes while I moored the boat to let the brothers cast their nets, I went into a deep slumber and once even slumped forward and fell down in the boat. Every night we splashed around on the river and did not return till 3:00 or 4:00 A.M., and then the next night we called out to each other and went fishing again.

When the base area and the province organization were relatively well established, the Province Party Committee met and discussed the policy of dispersing its members and sending each of them to a separate district to reinforce the leadership of the lower levels, cling tightly to the people, intensify the guerrilla warfare movement, and expand the liberated zone, following the example of the 3rd Zone in the delta of the North. So, everyone enthusiastically left the forest. I was sent to Mỏ Cày District. At that time, there was not a single liberated village left in this district. This area was devoid of forest and consisted entirely of rice fields and orchards. The cadres stayed there to operate, right in the midst of the people. In this situation where they had lost all areas under their control, the District Party Committee was very poor and their operating funds consisted of a mere one hundred piastres. We relied on the people for support.

Enemy repression was fiercer than ever before. Within a short time, one by one, the Secretary of the District Party Committee, the commander of the District Local Force, and a relatively large number of village and hamlet cadres were either killed in combat or captured and liquidated by the enemy. I myself came close to being killed many times. On January 15, 1952, I went with comrades Mười Phụ, Rô, and Phương who was the head of the District Office (Văn Phòng Huyện) to a site where a conference for Village Party Secretaries was being convened. In this period, the organization of the resistance at the basic levels had expanded. On the way, we stopped in to see the mother of a Village Party Secretary who had recently sacrificed his life. In the early morning hours, we were surrounded by the enemy conducting a sweep operation, and there was no way we could escape from the encirclement. The old lady took us to a secret underground hideout. When we reached the opening, comrade Phương hesitated and did not want to go down. He told me:

—You go down, I'll go outside to take a look.

Then he sneaked to the rice fields. About an hour later, the noose tightened around my hideout. Sitting inside I could hear clearly the voice of the officer cursing loudly. Their field radios exchanged messages full of code words such as goose, chicken, duck, tomato, big fish, small fish, etc. I asked myself, "How can I hear them so clearly from here?" I gave a sudden start when I saw that the lid of the bunker was opened a crack. The soldiers were searching around and making vague threats:

—If you don't come out, we'll shoot you to death!

I suddenly heard many shouts:

—Việt Minh! Việt Minh! Fire! Fire!

Bang, bang, bang!

—He bit the dust!

My head began to swim. I did not know whether it was comrade Phương or some other comrade who had just sacrificed his life, because a few embankments from where I was there was another bunker where Mười Phụ, a District Party Committee member, and Rô, the secretary of the District Party Committee office, were hiding. I hastily took out the documents and the sum of three thousand piastres which I was carrying, wrapped them in a piece of plastic, and buried it deep in the mud beneath the spot where I was sitting. Then I picked up some mud and smeared it all over myself. I listened attentively. Suddenly there was a noise right on top of my head and then a shaft of light shone into the bunker. The soldiers yelled: "A bunker, fire!" Not hesitating for one second, I tied my hair up in a topknot and tried to call out calmly:

—Please pull me out, young men! I'm just a woman hiding down here.

They pointed their rifles into the bunker and shouted. I climbed out, pretending to shake with fright so as not to arouse their suspicion. They asked me threateningly:

—Is there anyone else down there?

—There's no one else but me. I heard you firing so fiercely that I became scared and hid down there.

A cross-eyed fellow, rifle in hand, menacingly came over to frisk me. Finding in my pockets two hundred piastres and a fake identity card, he threw the paper on the ground and pocketed the two hundred piastres. He pretended to shout in anger:

—Hey you, Việt Minh! Where is your weapon? Did you leave it down in the bunker?

—I'm telling you the truth, I live and work here. I was frightened by the firing and hid in the bunker. I don't know anything about weapons.

He lunged and gave me a painful blow with his rifle butt:

—You still want to argue? If I find anything when I go down there I'll shoot you on the spot.

They looked around, but found no evidence. They told each other that they would have to beat me awhile to make me confess. Thereupon the four of them surrounded me menacingly on four sides. They beat me and kicked me without let up, and hit me with their rifle butts, while asking me constantly where the Việt Minh office and the troops were located. I gritted my teeth to bear the pain and repeated what I had told them. The same cross-eyed fellow stared at me lecherously and then winked to another fellow:

—Let's take her to the "boss"!

I shuddered when I heard his brazen words. With his rifle butt he shoved me inside a house nearby to meet his "boss," a fat and rotund man with a purple nose like a coagulated glob of blood in the middle of his face. The commander growled:

— Việt Minh cadre? If you don't confess, I'll shoot you and bury you on the spot.

I repeated what I had said before. He pointed his rifle away from me and told the soldier:

—Take her out and make her wash up, and then bring her back here.

A chill ran down my spine. I was terrified by his vile intention. How could I escape from being raped? I glanced toward the fence and saw the silhouette of an old woman. Suddenly an inspiration came to me and I shouted loudly:

—Mother, I've been arrested, please come in and ask them to release me so I can go back to my child.

The old woman was extremely brave. She ran over, her face distorted with weeping and scolded me:

—What kind of a daughter are you that you don't listen to me! I told you to stay home. Where did you go to get yourself arrested miserably like this

She went to stand in front of the commander and pleaded cleverly:

—Sir, my daughter is an innocent person, please let her go back to take care of her child.

The commander, his plan foiled, said angrily:

—This girl is a genuine Việt Minh caught in a secret bunker. We'll throw her in jail and keep her there till her bones rot, and we'll put you in jail too!

He screamed at the soldier:

—You, lock up these two haridans!

The soldier shoved me and the old woman. Suddenly, whistles blew. The soldiers hurriedly called out to each other to assemble. It seemed that this group had been ordered to reinforce another column that had come under attack. The commander ran around, screaming and cursing the soldiers like a vicious dog. Taking advantage of the confusion, the old woman and I ran into the garden and then crawled into a thick bush. The soldiers did not look for us. I looked at the old mother sitting next to me, and words choked in my throat.

* * *

The situation in Nam Bộ (South Vietnam) gradually changed for the better. In the Winter-Spring campaign at the end of 1953 and the beginning of 1954, in coordination with the Điện Biên Phủ battlefield, guerrilla warfare in the South erupted violently. The atmosphere was not unlike the effervescence of the August

Revolution and even appeared more decisive. The people thunderously swept away thick clumps of military posts. In many posts and watch towers, when they heard our rifle shots the soldiers yelled with panic: "Hey fellows, we're in for another Điện Biên Phủ!"

The liberated zone became very vast. In line with the directives of the higher levels, in each area that was liberated we immediately proceeded to distribute rice fields to the people. The entire membership of the Province Party Committee and of the District Party Committees—with the exception of those who were performing combat duties—plunged into the countryside. 1954 was a good harvest year. The peasants were simultaneously given the land and allowed to keep all their crops. Many villagers told me with tears in their eyes: "Only the Party and old Mr. Hồ have taken care of us like this."

We were winning big when the cease-fire order was issued. The Province Party Committee assigned me to explain our victory in the Geneva Accord. I met a unit surrounding a post. They received the cease-fire order when they could have taken it simply by firing a few shots. The entire unit had to withdraw. When they met me they were still frustrated and annoyed.

After I completed my task, I went back to meet Hai Tri and my son On in the Bến Tre province capital to discuss our family going to the North. We were reunited for the first time after five years. We talked about going or staying over and over again. On had grown and was now like a bird which had grown wings and feathers and wanted to fly away. He was very anxious to go to the North to study, while the brothers in the Bến Tre City Party Committee wanted me to allow him to stay with them because he was then doing mobilization work among the students and was a very good liaison agent in the city. On did not want to stay, and he often told me: "No matter what, you must let me go with you." Psychologically every mother wants to be close to her children. However, because I was thinking of his future I was determined to send him to the North, even if I stayed In the South, so he could study and make progress and later continue the unfinished work of his father. This was the most ardent aspiration I had for my beloved and unique son.

At that time, Hai Tri, my husband, was ill. He understood my maternal love and counseled me to go North with On. Frankly, I wanted very much to have my husband regroup to the North with On, so that he too would have the opportunity to study and to obtain medical treatment for his illness. Besides, he had never had the chance to visit the North. In the end, both of us stayed and only On left. I accompanied him for three or four days on the trip from Bến Tre all the way to the site of regroupment, Cà Mau. This was the first opportunity in eight or nine years that mother and son could spend such a long time together, confiding in each other and discussing all the affairs, big and small, of the family. In this situation, the greatest comfort for me was the sincere and moving words the villagers had said to me: "To have you, brothers and sisters, stay means we'll have the Party with us. If you all go, the enemy will soon slaughter us and to whom can we turn for help then?"

PART THREE

VII

There are two seasons in the South, the dry season and the rainy season. But under the regime of Ngô Đình Diệm, the henchman of the American imperialists, the people were battered by wind and rain all year around. Because of the [repression], after peace returned my husband and I had to part in order to continue to struggle alongside the people and force the enemy to correctly implement the Geneva Accords.

In this period, I had to disguise myself and raise pigs and poultry in the house of a villager, located in the middle of a field in an area bordering on three villages: Tân Hòa, Thạnh Phú Đông, and Phước Long. One afternoon, as the hour of my appointment with comrade Bảy, a local cadre, drew near, I suddenly saw a couple of people carrying bags like our liaison agents, approaching from the direction of the rice fields. I was suspicious and immediately thought of a way to cope with them. Without hesitating, I tied my hair in a topknot, rolled my pants up to my knees, put a betel wad in my mouth, and chewed slowly. I waited till they came close and then quietly carried a cauldron full of bran from the house to the pigsty. The three strangers approached and their arrogant and rude air showed clearly that they were not decent people. I asked first in a kind tone of voice:

—What business has brought you to my house, young gentlemen?

The fellow in front who had a long scar on his left cheek, opened wide his eyes [in a menacing manner] and said rudely:

—Do you have any pure-bred cocks to sell?

—We only have pigs and ducks.

The three of them slowly moved away. Two went straight into the house while the scar-faced fellow came over and stood near the pigsty, stared at me unblinkingly, and asked:

—Do you come from this area?

—Yes, my husband and I used to live in the village but we moved and built our house out here because it's easier to raise pigs and poultry here.

—Where's your husband?

—He's gone off to tend the ducks.

After I said it I became worried. If the owner of the house came back now and, unaware of the situation, addressed me as "sister" as usual, I would be in trouble because the attitude of these wolves had clearly betrayed what they were. I was also concerned that my appointment hour with brother Bảy had arrived. I still had not managed to think of a way to warn him. I looked out and saw that Bảy had taken a short cut and was at the gate. I immediately turned around and said loudly:

—Brother Bảy, these young gentlemen want to buy pure-bred cocks, if you have any take them to your home and sell them a couple.

He seemed to catch my meaning and immediately declined:

—If I had any chickens at home I wouldn't have come all the way here. I must ask you to sell me a duck so I can get ready for the anniversary of my mother's death.

The scar-faced fellow opened wide his eyes and looked at Bảy:

—Where do you live? Why did you have to come [all the way here] to buy ducks?

—I live in Cái Mít.

—What do you do in Cái Mít?

—I'm teaching children there.

The three of them surrounded him. One of them demanded:

—Show me your identity paper.

In this period, the people were forced by Ngô Đình Diệm to report one by one to the authorities who then issued each of them a different type of identification paper, depending on each individual. The "A" ID cards indicated people who were on their side; the "B" ID cards indicated those who were "Việt Cộng" suspects; and the "C" ID cards indicated genuine "Việt Cộng," that is to say all former members of the Resistance.

Asked about his paper, Bảy went pale but then immediately came up with an answer:

—I left my card at home.

The scar-faced fellow pierced Bảy with a fierce look and raged:

—One look at your face is enough to tell me what you are. Let's take him to the post, we don't have to waste any more time.

Bảy was stubborn and demanded that they take him home to get his ID card, hoping that he could manage to escape on the way. But the fellow loudly ordered the others to tie him up. I remained calm and told Bảy:

—Go to the post and try to bear it for a couple of days. I'll tell your wife what's happened and she'll come to fetch you back.

I meant to tell him in this manner not to give any information even if he was tortured. He replied:

—Yes, I'll try to bear it and I'll depend on your help.

It was thanks to my clever disguise and to the fact that I remained calm that they did not suspect me. Right after Bảy's arrest and before leaving to go to another area, I relayed the news to the comrades everywhere so that they would be on guard against the enemy searching for and capturing our basic level cadres.

It was also in this period that I received the news that my nephew Di, a cadre in Giồng Trôm district during the nine-year Resistance and the son of my brother, had recently been captured and murdered by the enemy. One day, at dusk, I stopped by my house in Hòa Thanh hamlet to find out more about Di's death and to check the situation. It was already dark but my mother had not stopped working and was still arduously digging up the earth. When she heard me calling her, she threw the pickaxe at the foot of an orange tree and said in a sad and angry tone of voice:

—I toil hard but in this kind of situation who knows whether I'll stay alive to enjoy the fruits of my labor.

She sighed with worry and asked me:

—Youngest one, you're back because you heard about Di, didn't you? You too, you must be careful.

Saying this, she covered her face and sobbed loudly. I felt choked with emotion.

That night, a niece of mine told me in detail about Di's glorious death. After peace returned, reactionaries who had taken up the priestly garb built a chapel in Lương Hòa village as a branch of the Ba Châu and Roman Church. On the day the chapel was inaugurated, Ngô—the parish priest—invited the villagers to attend. [During the ceremony] he stood up and made propaganda in front of the faithful, distorting the truth. He said that the Lord had brought peace and then praised "President Ngô" as the number one patriotic resistant.

Di was there that day. During the nine years of Resistance, Di was the Chairman of the Village Resistance Administrative Committee and the Secretary of the Village Party Committee. He had braved a lot of hardships to work for the people so they all loved and trusted him. Di let the priest finish and then stood up to point out the truth which contradicted everything the priest had said. Peace was restored only because the people of the entire country had fought for nine years. Only the Government of the Democratic Republic of Vietnam headed by Mr. Hồ Chí Minh led the national resistance against the French and brought it to victory. As for Ngô Đình Diệm, he was living in America in those years, getting fat on good food. He was not even in Vietnam, so how could he have been in the Resistance? The people were very pleased with what Di said and applauded loudly. The Priest had to shut up and no longer dared to tell lies.

From then on, Di withdrew into clandestine operations. But in April 1958 he was surrounded and captured by the enemy in Xóm Củi. They locked him up in Lương Quới and tortured him violently. They questioned him:

—Why didn't you regroup [to the North]? Why did you stay behind to sabotage the peace? Who else stayed behind with you?

Di accused them in return:

—I'm a former member of the Resistance. I fought the French to win peace and independence, I haven't committed any crimes. It's you who follow the Americans, it's you who have sold out the South to them, [and it's you] who have killed and harmed patriotic people. It's you who are sabotaging the Geneva Accords.

Other than that he did not say anything else. Seeing that they had failed to break this young but heroic cadre with torture, the enemy took him and locked him up in the Province Security Police office. Here, Di continued to heroically denounce Ngô Đình Diệm as a henchman of the American imperialists who had sabotaged the Geneva Accords. When he heard the news of Di's arrest, Ngô—the parish priest—plotted with the province chief to liquidate this cadre of the resistance. One night, they brought a Jeep to the prison door and dragged Di away. All the brothers in jail knew they were taking Di away to liquidate him, so they struggled to keep him back. Di also put up a fierce fight and refused to go, but being bare handed in such a situation what could he and the other prisoners do against a bloodthirsty gang with weapons in their hands. So they dragged Di to the car, drove him to Cầu Ván bridge on the Lương Hòa road, and shot him there in order to dampen our struggle movement. When they heard the shots, the villagers lit torches and poured out. The enemy panicked and fled. Di was not dead then. He calmly comforted his family and the people surrounding him:

—Please mother, friends, do not weep, and listen to me. They're very inhumane and cruel. They tortured me and tried to force me to give them information on the basic level organizations. But they did not get anywhere so they took me away to kill me in order to frighten you and make you afraid to oppose them. Don't be afraid, our revolution will certainly win. Take me to the province town so I can struggle and expose their crimes.

So, in the middle of the night, the people carried Di to the Lương Hòa post and then to the province town. All along the way Di condemned the enemy and appealed to the people to struggle with determination. Oblivious to the unrestrained and painful blows of the enraged enemy, Di continued to curse them without letup until he could talk no more.

The situation everywhere became more gloomy. Right in my native village at this time, the Diệm clique established a Council of Notables and set up Phán, a notorious tyrant, as Chairman. They built two large posts at both ends of the village. Their henchmen—from the militiamen to the secret and regular police—came from landlord families and were a bunch of crooks and tyrants. They aggressively searched each house, weapons in hand, and demanded that the people deliver paddy to the landlords. If they suspected someone of being a Việt Cộng, they arrested and murdered him without flinching, as they had murdered my nephew.

All of Bến Tre province lived in this oppressive and suffocating atmosphere. Many patriotic people were rounded up, taken away, and liquidated. We immediately thought that in order to survive we would have to consolidate and expand our ranks for the struggle, otherwise if we let the masses remain quiet, dispersed, and unorganized, we would all perish. This was the common determination shared by every patriotic person in the South. The collective leadership assigned a number of comrades and me to shoulder part of this critical and glorious mission.

After taking part in laying down a program of action with the other comrades in Bình Đại, I moved to Châu Thành district to operate. Comrade Thanh Hà, the key cadre of the district, took me to a secret site to discuss our activities. He told me angrily:

—That wretched Tức (a leading cadre of the province) has been arrested and he's spilled out everything to the enemy. He's now guiding the security police to track you down relentlessly.

He then showed me a leaflet bearing my picture and the following words printed in huge letters: "Reward of 10,000 piastres to anyone who can apprehend Nguyễn Thị Định, an extremely dangerous 'Việt Cộng female'. She is fat, has a fair complexion, thick eyebrows, wavy hair and a birthmark on the right cheek." After I read the leaflet I burst out laughing:

—Their description of me is quite accurate, don't you think so, Comrade Hà?

He was amused and added:

—Do you know what else they're forcing the people to do to worship them and to help them capture us alive?

Then he ticked off on his fingers:

(a) A flag with three bars[13]
(b) A small wooden block[14]

---

[13] This refers to the national flag of the Republic of South Vietnam which has three red bars against a yellow background. The expression used, "cờ ba sọc," is a sarcastic and pejorative way of referring to the Sài Gòn flag. *Trans.*

(c) A length of rope
(d) A sharpened stick
(e) A torch

—Every family must have these five things on hand.

Hà, a former high school student who was always cheerful and loved to banter, then added:

—Their plan is so foolproof we won't be able to escape, don't you agree?

Then he laughed uproariously. I added my opinion:

—But our people have been led and educated by our Party; they've fought for nine years, and they know who are their friends and who are their enemies, so no matter what devilish tricks the enemy can come up with, they won't be able to do anything to us.

While discussing the mission and integrity of a revolutionary, comrade Thanh Hà pledged:

—If I'm arrested I wont give any information to the enemy—even if I have to die. Damn that fellow Tức, only a character like him can be so wretched.

I agreed completely:

—Me too. We must encourage each other to maintain our standpoint and integrity. If a cadre confesses anything to the enemy at this point, he'll cause great damage to the revolution, demoralize the people and make them lose faith in the revolution.

After completing my work with comrade Hà, I had just gone a few hundred meters from the meeting site when dozens of security policemen burst into the house where Hà was staying. I went into a pagoda and pretended to be a worshipper. The agent who had gone to check the situation came back and informed me that Hà had managed to hide in his secret hideout when the security police arrived. However, the policemen saw women's clothing in the house and suspected that I was around. They arrested the owner of the house, beat him up, and found the secret shelter. They tortured comrade Hà brutally. During these severe beatings, blood gushed from his nose and mouth, but he gritted his teeth and bore the pain, and did not moan or utter a word.

I quickly relayed the news to every area so that our organizations could immediately expose the crime of the enemy, incite profound hatred among the masses against the enemy, and so that they would continue to nurture and expand the reliable grassroot bases of the revolution. At the same time the higher levels also issued a similar directive and reminded us to absolutely withdraw into

---

[14] The villagers were supposed to knock on the wooden block to alert government authorities of any communist presence in the village. *Trans.*

clandestine action, live in secret hideouts, travel and operate entirely at night.

I left that evening, disguised as a nun, in the company of a novice of the pagoda who was about fifteen years old. The two of us walked for a long time and finally at three o'clock in the morning arrived at another basic level organization to meet comrade Tùng, a district cadre. From then on, comrade Tùng and I resolutely contacted people and set up grassroot bases. During those extremely difficult years filled with hardships, like all the other comrades, I had to hide and sleep in the bushes, but the people did their best to protect and help us. One night, comrade Tùng and I were sleeping in a garden in Phú An Hòa village. It was already ten o'clock but the barking of dogs in the settlement was getting fiercer and fiercer—starting first far away and then spreading closer and closer—and then we heard the scream of a woman. A while later, a person came and informed us that Mrs. Nam, our liaison agent, who was operating overtly under legal cover, had been arrested. The enemy tortured her brutally and asked her where we were but she adamantly said she did not know. They beat her till they broke both of her legs, but still could not break the iron will of a human being who had discarded her own life to protect the revolution. I haven't heard any news about her and do not know whether she is still alive or dead.

Also, while in this area, comrade Tùng and I once made a trip from Phú An Hòa village to Phước Thạnh village, near the An Hòa canal, to reach the house of a woman who was a sympathizer. Not daring to walk on the road for fear of running into the enemy, we waded in the irrigation ditches running along the orchards. The night was as black as ink, and it was raining in a drizzle, but we kept having to climb out of one ditch into another, and our legs became rubbery with fatigue. Once, I bumped my head against a coconut tree that had fallen across the ditch and a huge bump swelled on top of my head. Once in a while I pitched forward and fell into the ditch, my chest hitting the embankment, and I became numb with pain. Tùng had to lead me by the hand part of the way, as though he was guiding a blind woman. We picked our way through the darkness and walked from 7:00 P.M. till 3:00 A.M. when we finally reached the house of a hard-core sympathizer. His family consisted of himself, his wife, and their two children. Thành, the girl, was thirteen years old, and Công, the boy, was five years old. After we finished eating, it was already daylight. Comrade Tùng went to stay with another family. Mr. and Mrs. Tư left to work in the fields, leaving Thành to watch the house. I was exhausted and overslept. At around 10:00 A.M., dogs started to bark from afar and then the barking spread closer. Thành ran out to take a look and then ran back, her face ashen with fear, and said in a panic:

—Soldiers are coming, Miss Năm!

I quickly calmed her down:

—Nothing will happen, keep calm. I'll go down into the secret hideout, close the cover after me.

As I talked, I lifted the cover and jumped down. Water in the hole sloshed and overflowed. It was a dangerous situation, but there was nothing better I could do. Thành who was quick witted poured the pot full of cooked bran for feeding the pigs over the shelter cover. The pot broke, the bran splattered everywhere and covered the opening of the shelter. She slapped Công's face and said:

—You broke the pot of bran, when mother comes back she'll beat you to death, you'll see!

Poor Công did not understand anything and the painful blow made him wail. Right at that moment, dozens of soldiers entered and saw Công crying and the pot of bran broken to pieces. Thành nodded in greeting and then continued to scold her brother. The soldiers stood around, asked a few questions, and then left. I heaved a sigh of relief and greatly admired Thành's brilliant idea. After the soldiers had gone a long time, I got out of the shelter, took both children in my arms and told them softly:

—You two saved my life.

The day I left, Thành did not want to let me go. She wept pitifully and kept asking me to take her along.

At this time, the enemy was hunting down and arresting cadres relentlessly. One after another, five of the leading district cadres were arrested. The higher levels sent comrade Sáu Quân to replace Thanh Hà. The situation was very gloomy. The hounds—security policemen and informers—were poking around everywhere. At night, the villages were deserted and dead quiet since every family was forbidden to go out and had to stay indoors. When cadres came back to visit, the villagers wept bitterly and said:

—The revolution must do something, otherwise if things go on like this you brothers and sisters will all be arrested and murdered.

In this period, it was extremely difficult for us to find a place to stay. Our old hideouts had been discovered, and though we had set up new ones we did not dare to go there either. Having no other alternative, comrade Sáu Quân and I discussed withdrawing to Lương Phú village, in Giồng Trôm district, an area which the enemy had not paid much attention to. However, our grassroot bases there were still very sparse. We stayed in the house of one of my sisters, right next to the Lương Phú post and across from the Lương Hòa post. A few days later we moved in with a new sympathizer, a very kind old lady who took care of a pagoda. But a few days after we got there the hounds picked up our scent. One day, brother Sáu Quân and I were staying in the private quarters of this lady when up to a platoon of security policemen suddenly appeared, surrounded the pagoda, and burst inside the house to search. Thanks to a secret shelter underneath the Buddhist altar we escaped death. Not finding us in the pagoda, the enemy searched and interrogated the houses next door. Sáu Quân and I had to quickly find a way to get out of the area. It was the middle of the day. Taking advantage of a moment when the enemy let down their guard, Sáu Quân crawled into the garden and then climbed and hid at the top of a coconut tree. Unfortunately I could not climb, so I hastily put on some Buddhist nun's garments, disguised myself as a novice, and, in the company of a thirteen year old novice, sneaked to a sampan and took the risk of rowing away in search of another grassroot base. In the end, I took the risk of returning to Hòa Thạnh hamlet, Lương Hòa village where I was born. This was where I had operated when I first started to work for the revolution. Here I would be close to my family. I was confident that the people would protect me, even though this area—and in particular my family and relatives—were under tight enemy surveillance. After ten years, when they suddenly saw me return in this extremely tense situation, many villagers were so scared that they went white with fear. But just a couple of days later I succeeded in persuading five or six families to accommodate us—these were all families of very poor peasants. Thanks to this, the district leadership organ gradually shifted here to guide the movement.

After the affairs of Giồng Trôm and Châu Thành districts had been relatively stabilized, I transferred to Mỏ Cày district to operate. Upon my arrival I saw comrades Tám Chữ, Ba Đào, Hai Thủy, Ba Kiên, and Hai Lân and we immediately held a meeting to discuss a plan to oppose Diệm's "national day" (October 26, 1959). The collective [leadership] assigned me to lead the movement in Mỏ Cày district. We dispersed right that night. However, I had to stay behind because my guide had not arrived. When night came it began to rain. Seeing that I was by myself and that I had had a hard journey, Tư, his wife, and his mother urged me to spend the night in the house. The old lady said:

—Sleep here and go in the morning. Nothing will happen to us, my child.

I was moved by her noble sentiment toward the revolution. Although Diệm had issued the 10/59 decree which stipulated that if a "Việt Cộng" cadre was found in any house, the owner would be thrown in jail and his property confiscated, the people were not afraid. On the contrary, they continued to love and protect the cadres as before. However, to guard against anything unexpected which might happen, I adamantly asked them to let me go and sleep outside near the secret hideout. As the night advanced, the wind became chilly and I felt numb with cold. I was sitting all hunched up near the shelter when suddenly I heard dogs barking loudly. I noticed that my heart started to beat wildly because in that period the barking of dogs at night signaled that soldiers were searching for our people. Suddenly I saw crisscrossing beams of flashlights and heard shouts and thudding sounds of beating coming from Tư's house. I knew the enemy was on our trail and hastily climbed into the bunker. Unfortunately the rain had clogged the air vent with mud. Sitting in the bunker for a while I began to feel dizzy and almost passed out. I had to climb out and crawl to the sugarcane field where I covered myself with leaves. I spent all that day lying in the sugarcane field. I was soaking wet but did not dare to go back to the house because the liaison agent had not come to contact me. Besides, it was impossible to leave at this point. I lay there, reviewing in my mind each and every grassroot base. More than half of the hard-core sympathizers had been uncovered. Our survival depended on whether or not we could expand the number of sympathizers. We had often told each other that unless we held on to the people we could not maintain the movement. This was the most critical problem. I thought of going to the house of a very good relative of mine in order to contact the people and recruit a number of sympathizers. However, I recalled the recent story of comrade Chiến going to the house of one of his relatives, and this put me on my guard.

One time, comrade Chiến, who was in charge of Thạnh Phú district, was traveling in the company of another comrade. When they were close to his house, they found themselves caught in an enemy operation. Chiến escaped, but the other comrade was killed. The enemy searched his wallet and found pictures of both himself and Chiến, which they posted at the communal house and claimed they had killed two "Việt Cộng." Chiến hid in the rice fields until nightfall and then picked his way through the darkness to the house of his aunt. Chiến knocked on the door and announced himself, but his aunt started to shout:

—I don't have any relatives! Go away!

Chiến knew she was afraid it was an enemy agent pretending to be her relative in order to test her. However, if he lingered there and the hamlet chief found out, he would be in danger. So he turned around and left, feeling sad and angry at the enemy who had driven even relatives to suspect one another.

It was dark again. I was deep in thought trying to find some ways to consolidate and expand the movement when I heard footsteps approaching the secret hideout and someone calling softly:

—Ba, my child, it's me, mother. I've brought you something to eat.

I ran toward her, and before I could comfort her and shore up her spirit, she said:

—They've arrested Tư, but I'm not worried because you and the others are all right. Even if that scoundrel Diệm arrests and kills me, I won't abandon you.

Her words warmed my heart. I forgot about the cold and clasped her hands tightly:

—You're right, mother. No matter what the Diệm gang does they won't be able to stamp out the revolution. One of these days they will have to answer for their crimes in front of the people.

Suddenly I thought of the folk poem I had memorized long ago:

"The people's hearts are like sunflowers
Hundreds of thousands of them all turn toward the sun.
    Even if everything in nature changes
They pledge to remain steadfast and loyal to the revolution."

VIII

During those dark and gloomy years in the South, the American-Diệm gang did their best to suppress and kill patriotic people. They did not hesitate to use any schemes, no matter how savage [to achieve their aims] and created untold sufferings and miseries for the women.

I still remember comrade Biên, a company cadre who asked me before he regrouped to the North to take care of Chín, his wife, a good sympathizer in the village. Chín was still young, only about twenty years old, and had a tanned complexion. She was not beautiful but was very charming. She was childless and lived by herself. When we met for the first time she said:

— Biên loves me a lot and so even if our separation lasts for a hundred years I'll wait for him.

I guided her into becoming a very reliable supporter.

Nhí, the daughter of a landlord, lived in the same village. She had small, beady eyes which were constantly darting flirtatious glances at the men. She was also married to a military cadre who had regrouped to the North. Half in jest, half seriously, she once asked Chín:

—How long do you think you can wait for your husband?

As people say, "children take after their parents." After the Diệm gang came into power, they set up Nhí's father—a landlord—as the hamlet chief. During the *ly khai* (renunciation of communism) campaign[15] the Americans and Diệm forced the women whose husbands had regrouped to the North to announce that they had rejected their husbands and severed their allegiance to the "Việt Cộng." They even invented a ceremony during which those who had made the renunciation were "accepted into the fold." Prompted by her father, Nhí volunteered to come forward and declare that she had severed her allegiance to the "Việt Cộng" represented by her husband, to marry a puppet lieutenant with a mouth filled with gold teeth. The two of them went to the city to have clothes made. When she came back, Nhí was wearing a transparent and skintight nylon blouse and bouffant hairdo which looked like an owl's nest. Nhí went to see Chín and poured honeyed words into her ears:

—My girl, life's not very long. If we don't live it up we'll miss a lot of things and we'll grow old before we know it.

Chín was kind to the buddha but not to the devil. She insulted her to her face:

—Only you can entertain such thoughts. I haven't lost my conscience and cannot betray my husband's love, as you've done.

Nhí accepted defeat because she could not make Chín change her mind. Next came the turn of a policeman wearing a dangling Colt pistol who came to court Chín and persuade her to become his concubine. Chín refused. He then changed his tune and gave her two choices:

—You either follow the nationalists or support the communists, you must choose one of these two roads.

---

[15] This was a campaign launched by Diệm to force former members of the Resistance to renounce their allegiance to the Việt Minh. The penalty for refusing to go along was imprisonment, torture, and sometimes execution. For a very vivid and informative description of this campaign see Nguyễn Đức Thuận, *Bất Khuất* (Indomitable) (Hà Nội: Thanh Niên, 1967). The author was tortured and thrown into the tiger cage at Côn Sơn for refusing to renounce his allegiance. *Trans.*

Chín replied:

—What does the love between a wife and husband have anything to do with the nationalists, why should I make the choice?

He tried to trap her:

—If you want to go to the North to rejoin your husband, I'll ask the nationalists to let you go.

Chín answered cleverly:

—It's up to the nationalists. Which woman doesn't want to rejoin her husband?

He grimaced:

—Don't you know that the French boat which carried the regroupees capsized and sank in the open seas and everyone aboard drowned? Why waste time waiting?

—I'll decide what to do when I know for certain my husband's dead.

He became threatening:

—Let me tell you, the nationalists are about to march to the North and sweep away all the communists. There's no doubt about that. You watch out!

Poor Chín, she was entirely on her own so how could she cope with this band of tigers craving for human flesh? I thought of transferring her to another area, but one night the policeman came and arrested her right in her house. She struggled and scratched his face but he did not let go. He raped her and then stabbed her to death. However, even in death she was not left in peace. This brute slashed open her belly, cut out her gall bladder which he presented to the authorities [to support his] claim that he had killed a Việt Cộng in order to obtain a reward from that haridan Lệ Xuân.[16]

Besides Miss Chín, the wife of comrade Mười Văn was also most faithful. It was his wife's death which plunged me deep in thought. Mrs. Mười was a Southerner, simple, good hearted, and straightforward like thousands of other women. During the nine years of Resistance, her husband was away on mission for long stretches of time, dropping in to see his family once in a while when he had the chance and then going off again. On her own, she worked hard to support her children and contribute to the resistance. All her children, the boys as well as the girls, later left to work for the revolution. After peace returned, Mười and his children stayed behind with the people and did not regroup to the North. The enemy knew this and tracked them down relentlessly. Unable to find them, they came and arrested Mrs. Mười. They asked her:

—Where is your husband at this moment?

---

[16] Madame Ngô Đình Nhu's maiden name. *Trans.*

She maintained she did not know, though they beat her and tortured her brutally. Before dying, she pointed to her chest and screamed in their faces:

—My husband and my children are lodged deep in my heart. If you wretches want to find them, you'll have to cut out my heart and look inside.

The heroic sacrifice of Mrs. Mười expressed the indomitable fighting spirit of thousands of women in the South. I used the examples of Mrs. Mười and Chín to educate the other women. While I was mobilizing their spirits and deepening their hatred [of the Sài Gòn authorities], [among the women] was Hạnh, a girl from Thạnh Phú district who was then about twenty-three or twenty-four years old. She was beautiful but did not want to get married. Whenever anyone asked her about this, she simply said:

—I must take part in the resistance first.

Once when she met me she said with determination:

—If I find myself in the same situation as sisters Mười and Chín, I'm sure I can do as well as they did.

Later, Hạnh was captured by the enemy while she was operating in the district. Seeing that Hạnh was beautiful they tried to entice her with every means at their disposal, but she did not change her mind. The famished wolves then resorted to brutal acts. They stripped her naked, tied her up, and employed all their savage tricks. They even rubbed hot pepper into her vagina, but failed to break this heroic girl. Several of them broke beer bottles, thrust the necks into her, pulled out the bloody things, raised them up and laughed. They tortured her for a long time without success, so they took her to see Tức, a traitor who had surrendered to the enemy, and had him try to persuade her. The moment she saw this scoundrel, she spat in his face and cursed him:

—You wretched traitor and surrenderer (*đầu hàng*).

Tức bowed his head and did not dare to look her in the eyes. The enemy tortured Hạnh violently and tenaciously for six continuous months. Hạnh was reduced to a skeleton covered with skin. She lay immobile, paralyzed, and could only move her fingers and talk in whispers. However, she did not stop cursing Diệm and the Americans.

Another person who used insults as a weapon to strike at the Americans and Diệm in this period was Mrs. Năm in Minh Đức whom people used to call "Mrs. Năm, the daughter of old Mr. Hồ" (*bà Năm con cụ Hồ*) because this was the name she gave herself. Singing was the main expression of her mental disorder. Every night she got up at three or four o'clock and sang till daylight. She was crazy but also lucid because her songs had a clear content. She insulted from Ngô Đình Diệm down to the landlord, the hamlet chief, and the tyrannical militiamen, but she always praised the revolution and President Hồ. In 1958, she was over fifty years old. She was very emaciated but had a strong and loud voice. During nights when the wind was still, people living two kilometers away could hear her curses.

Her family was poor. Her husband caught fish which she took to the market to sell. After selling her fish, she usually stayed at the market and cursed until it broke up. On the way back, wearing a white towel wrapped around her neck and carrying a basket containing betel leaves and areca nuts, she called out Diệm's name and cursed him as she walked, all the way home. At the beginning the enemy arrested her and beat her up, but this only made her curse them even more. A woman like Mrs. Năm who had been abused by the landlords and imperialists and who had had to work as a servant at the age of ten had become oblivious to physical pains. At the market when the enemy forced everyone to salute the flag, she turned her back and said:

—Salute my ass!

On the way back, passing by the post, she asked the guard:

—Are you selling pigs here?

The sentry replied "No" and motioned her to move with his rifle butt. She cursed him:

—Damn your ancestors! If this isn't a pigsty, why all this careful fencing then?

The guard raised his rifle and threatened her:

—Do you know what this is?

—What is it? It's what you get for selling your country, what else can it be?

The soldiers in the post poured out, surrounded her, and forced her to sing. She set down a condition:

—Damn the ancestors of those who beat me up because of what I sing!

She immediately launched into a song. The lyrics rhymed beautifully and were insults directed at Ngô Đình Diệm. One time the soldiers met her in the market. They showed her a leaflet bearing a cartoon of President Hồ, drawn to look extremely emaciated, in order to falsely show that people in the North were starving. They teased her:

—Isn't your father eating at all, why is he so thin?

She immediately got mad:

—Yeah, my father is so consumed with worry about the welfare of the country that he's lost weight. He's not like Ngô Đình Diệm who's eaten so much of the leftover milk and butter of the Americans that he's become as fat as a sow about to have a litter.

The comrades used her house as an operating base. One evening they took Ba Đào, Ba Cấu, and me there. She showed us into a room in the back. Seeing two fat comrades she asked right away:

—Are you landlords?

Before they could answer, she said:

—Landlords like you are all right.

Ba Đào asked her:

—Why?

—You're all right because you have enough sense to join the revolution and work to make up for your crimes.

After that first meeting I had some doubts about her mental illness. The next day, we held a meeting in the room. She puttered around in the garden. Suddenly we heard Mrs. Năm ask a question and a man reply:

—Where are you going, young man?

—I'm on my way to buy rice seedlings.

—Whose land are you renting? Do you pay rent?

—The land belongs to the government, so I pay rent to the government.[17]

—You must be crazy! The land belongs to us people. It was given to us by Uncle Hồ. Where could the government have found an inch of land to call its own? If the Ngô Đình Diệm government doesn't have any rice to feed themselves, then let them feed on people's blood. Don't pay rent to them any more!

I was elated by what she said but had to suppress my laughter. A while later I heard Mrs. Năm speak again:

—Do you know how your President Diệm came into being?

—The Lord created him.

She gave a loud and prolonged hiss:

—He came out of a sow's ass! You don't know anything!

---

[17] This is a reference to communal land. *Trans.*

—A while ago, a security policeman showed his face here but I chased him away.

I started when I heard this and greatly admired her for her cleverness. Hers was the cleverness of a crazy woman whose madness was only directed at the enemy.

During the darkest years of the revolution in the South, it was people like Miss Chín, sister Mười Văn, mother Năm, and little Thành who taught me a very profound lesson about patriotism and the indomitable spirit of a revolutionary. It was this [spirit of patriotism and indomitability] which kept us from faltering and enabled us to stay by the side of the people, cling to the land, and resolutely maintain the movement without being deterred by hardships, dangers, and death.

IX

At the end of 1959, I was busily engaged in my work when I was urgently called to help provide guidance for dealing with the enemy's plot of setting up an agroville in Thành Thới village, Mỏ Cày district. The villagers were angry and up-in-arms because they had been ordered by Diệm and the Americans to tear down their houses and move within a month. An entire area of fertile rice fields, luxuriant fruit trees, and densely populated settlements—from the Rạch Bần arroyo to the Cầu Cống bridge, over ten kilometers in length—had to be completely evacuated for the establishment of an agroville. The enemy's plot was to assemble all families with relatives who had regrouped to the North and those of the cadres who had left to work for the revolution, and patriotic people, in this hell on earth.

Diệm and the Americans had chosen Thành Thới village as a testing ground to develop the experience which they would then apply all over the South. When they met us, the villagers said:

—If we're going to die, we're going to die right here, we're not going anywhere.

We were very happy to hear the people say this because only by relying on the unity and determination of the entire population could we foil the cruel scheme of the enemy. As anticipated, a month passed without any villagers obeying the order to dismantle their houses, although the enemy exerted intense pressure and blatantly resorted to force. Two companies under the command of Ba Hương were brought in and these then coordinated with two battalions from the 7th Division to blanket all neighboring villages. Every day, they set fire to houses, cut down trees, and crushed lush rice fields with tractors. The brutes poured toward the house of sister Tư. Her husband had been killed in action fighting for the Resistance. After the Điện Biên Phủ victory the revolution gave her three *công* of land to farm and support her five young children. After peace returned, she painstakingly built an embankment to grow tangerines, clod of earth by clod of earth. The tangerines were beginning to ripen when the soldiers came to cut them down. Watching them destroy what she had constructed with sweat and tears, she shouted in anger:

—Heavens above, what kind of government is this that can be so cruel?

Her children rushed in and tried to prevent the soldiers from cutting down the trees, but the soldiers were unmoved for they could not care less whether the people starved and died.

All the young people were conscripted to do forced labor, and anyone who resisted was arrested and jailed. Under the burning sun, about five thousand villagers—young and old, men and women—were gathered and forced to destroy hundreds of acres of lush rice plants already bearing young grains bursting with milky sap. The soldiers took measurements and as soon as they finished measuring the people would have to start digging. The villagers huddled together in one spot and refused to dig. A couple of old people came forward and protested:

—The government said it is concerned about the life of the people but hasn't done anything to prove it. Now it is forcing us to tear down our houses, destroy and burn our properties, dig up the graves of our ancestors, and perform exhausting corvee tasks. How are the people going to survive?

Ba Hương—a fellow notorious for his brutality—seeing that the people were protesting and refusing to work, picked up his whip, ran over menacingly, and lashed wildly at the villagers:

—You mother . . . how dare you resist the orders of the government? Where are the soldiers? Shoot immediately anyone who refuses to work.

Many people in this area had died from hunger, diseases, and the abuses of the soldiers. [For example, once] the soldiers entered the house of Miss Ch., pinned her to the ground, and took turns raping her until she passed out. [Another time] they entered An Lộc hamlet in broad daylight and raped a twelve-year-old girl who died from the profuse bleeding. Any villager who objected was accused of being a Việt Cộng. Phú—a local brute—once led Ba Hương's band into the village where they shot two twelve-year-old boys herding buffaloes, cut off the heads, and carried them back to the agroville to claim they had eliminated two dangerous Việt Cộng reconnaissance agents.

Motivated and guided by the cadres, the people from Thành Thới village and Mỏ Cày district joined forces with the villagers conscripted to perform corvee—forming a group about one thousand strong who moved forward en masse to present their demands to Ba Hương:

—We oppose forced labor!

—We demand compensation for damaged property and lost income!

—We demand that we be allowed to return to our old homes to farm and earn out living.

Hương roared:

—Did you listen to the urgings of the Việt Cộng and come here to struggle?

Mrs. Bảy stepped forward and said:

—Look, my husband and myself along with our nine children depend entirely on the income from our five *công* of fruit grove to live, now you've forced us to cut all the trees down. Then you forced my husband to do corvee work. You don't give him any rice to eat and beat him violently besides. Let me ask you, how is our family going to survive?

Hương lunged and kicked her in the stomach, and she fell rolling on the ground. He lashed her with his whip and cursed her:

—She's the leader, let me beat her one hundred lashes till she dies.

Then he ordered the soldiers to assault the people. The villagers screamed and protested violently, and rushed in to rescue Mrs. Bảy who had become unconscious, her body all black and blue from the beating. A little later she revived, looked at the people and said:

—Don't worry, I'm still alive. Just carry me to the district town to struggle and expose this gang.

As Tết drew near the Americans and Diệm intensified their pressure to have the agroville completed. They even brought in conscripted laborers from all six provinces of Central Nam Bộ to work on the agroville. Every day, more than ten thousand people lived at the site in extremely crowded conditions. The flames of hatred smoldered in the hearts of the people, ready to erupt at the right opportunity. One day, Ba Hương ordered the buildings spruced up to welcome Diệm who was coming to inspect the agroville. The villagers went looking for the cadres to relay the news and to solicit their opinion. On the appointed day, the soldiers beat the drums, making a dreadful din, searched each house, and forced the people to hang out flags and don new clothes to welcome "President Diệm." That day, I stayed close by to keep track of the situation. Following the cadres' instructions faithfully, the village notables—formally dressed, petitions hidden in the sleeves of their robes—stood in the front row. The villagers called out to each other to go and welcome the president, and with everyone bustling about, the atmosphere was very different from the one prevailing normally. The security police and the militia were overjoyed, convinced they would be rewarded for their work this time around.

That morning, wherever Diệm went, telephones rang to announce his movement. He went to Mỏ Cày, Thơm, and then arrived in Thành Thới. The moment his car came to a stop the villagers—defying the thick ring of security and regular police—took off the outer layer of clothing and appeared in ragged and filthy clothes. They wrapped their heads in mourning bands and rushed onto the road, moaning and weeping as though they were at a funeral. It was complete chaos. The policemen blew their whistles, tried to hold the people back with their rifle butts, and fired madly into the air, but could not prevent the ring of people from closing around Ngô Đình Diệm's car. The notables handed their petitions directly to Diệm, while the people handed theirs to the soldiers and reporters. Seizing this opportunity, many women and children clung to Diệm and the officers by hanging on to their jackets, weeping pitifully, and demanding the release of their husbands and parents. Ngô Đình Diệm, greatly embarrassed, stood up to make a few promises and then fled from the scene. After this defeat, at the orders of the Americans and Diệm, their lackeys took revenge on the people and launched a fierce wave of repression in Mỏ Cày district and all over Bến Tre province.

Also in this period Diệm concocted the 10/59 decree, an extremely fascist law under which anyone who entertained thoughts of opposition—even if he did not take any concrete action to oppose the regime—would be labeled Việt Cộng and guillotined. The mobile guillotine was taken everywhere and prisons mushroomed. Newspapers [controlled by Diệm] clamored for on-the-spot executions of Communists without hesitation. The brutality of Ngô Đình Diệm's reactionary regime was at its peak. Their desire now was to imprison all the patriotic people of Bến Tre province in the Thành Thới agroville, this hell on earth, and to liquidate the people of the South with the 10/59 decree and the guillotine.

The sympathetic villagers in Mỏ Cày district wept and told me:

—Sister, we must arm ourselves in order to survive, otherwise we'll die. If you permit us to kill the security police agents to obtain weapons, we'll do it right away. The Americans and Diệm have torn up the Geneva Accords long ago. We can't be kind to the devil! Whenever the call for armed resistance is issued, just let us know and we'll leave at once. If we go on like this, they'll burn down our houses and kill us one of these days. We won't have anything with which to fight back and it will be unbearable.

Whenever they ran into me the comrades from every district in the province impatiently asked:

—We heard that Hồng Ngự [District, Kiến Tường province] and Đồng Tháp [The Plain of Reeds] have taken up arms. How about our province? Have we been allowed to strike back?

I told them my true feeling:

—I share your wishes.

X

The time finally came when the ardent aspiration of our people and cadres was at last satisfied. I received a letter from the higher levels instructing me to attend a conference to hear a new and extremely important resolution. While helping me prepare [for the trip], the comrades in the Bến Tre leadership committee told me over and over again:

—Do your best to get there. No matter what the difficulties are, try by all means to bring back the new policy and transmit it to us, will you?

I understood the anxiety of the comrades and, aware of how eagerly they awaited the news, my enthusiasm and agitation intensified as I departed. On this trip there were two things which made me enthusiastic and eager: meeting the higher echelons to inform them of the aspirations of the masses, and finding out whether their policy conformed to the wishes of the people.

When I reached the conference site the first man I met was Bảy Ruộng. He asked me about the conditions in my locality and helped me gain a better understanding of the overall situation. We waited for almost a month before Sáu Đường finally returned from a meeting with the higher levels. When I met Sáu Đường, Hai Điền, and Ba Bổn and saw that they were all right I felt very happy. Sáu Đường had lost a lot of weight and looked very pale. These brothers had had to live out in the bushes and it was inevitable that they fell prey to diseases and became emaciated. Sáu Đường was always in a cheerful mood and every time I ran into him he told me countless stories about enthusiastic and burning struggles. He presided over the conference. Since peace was restored six years ago this was the first time that I attended such an important meeting. Sáu Đường gave a report on the current situation and the policy adopted by the higher levels. The moment he mentioned this policy I felt an immense joy and happiness. It clearly called for the mobilization of the people all over the South to carry out political struggle in conjunction with military action. The moment they heard military action mentioned the conference burst out in stormy applause. The higher levels had followed exactly the aspirations of the lower levels in an extraordinary manner. Seeing that the comrades were too enthusiastic about military action, Sáu Đường had to remind them over and over again:

—Comrades, please remember that political struggle is the main policy, armed action only supplements it and is aimed at mobilizing the peasants to rise up and destroy the enemy's suffocating control in order to become masters of the countryside, of their villages and hamlets.

When we discussed the favorable and unfavorable factors involved, I felt uneasy about the fact that we did not possess any weapons, and without weapons how were we going to combine [political action] with armed struggle? I boldly asked:

—Unless you give us some weapons we won't be able to combine [political struggle] with armed action.

Sáu Đường burst out laughing:

—Go back and tell the enemy to hand over their weapons for you to use. To tell the truth, even if we had weapons here you wouldn't be able to carry them back with you.

I answered stubbornly:

—Never mind, just give me the weapons and I'll find a way to take them back with me.

The day before I left, Sáu Đường came to see me and asked:

—As far as the policy to combine [political action] with armed struggle is concerned, do you think the cadres and people will go along with it?

—They'll be terribly pleased! Everyone has been waiting just for this.

I replied firmly:

—You're being subjective and ascribing your own inclination to others!

I was positive:

—I'm only afraid that once Bến Tre turns to military action we won't be able to restrain them.

He asked:

—What are your plans of action when you go back there?

The memory of the tumultuous days of the August 1945 Revolution suddenly came back to me. I told the comrades about my wish and dream: we would have to carry out a concerted uprising in order to achieve certain success. After I left the conference site, I had just gone a short distance when I ran into an enemy mop-up operation. I was stranded in the rice fields for a whole week. Each night I waded in the water and covered about ten kilometers without any food in my stomach. Every time I set foot in the rice fields, leeches came swarming all around. I felt very anxious, as though I was sitting on fire, afraid that the comrades from the other provinces would reach their destinations first and carry out the uprising without our province joining in, so that when our turn came the enemy would have taken their precautions.

I reached Trà Vinh exactly on December 30, 1959 and tried to contact the province leadership committee but they had moved elsewhere. The local infrastructure did not know where they had gone because the comrade in charge of the province liaison station had been arrested. I was worried and wondered who else had been captured. Recently, the enemy had jailed and killed four or five comrades in the province leadership committee, including Bùi Ngọc Nghi who was killed in Thạnh Phú less than a month ago.

I [decided to] go back to the house of Mrs. Năm —"old Mr. Hồ Chí Minh 's daughter"—in Minh Đức because Ngoan, her son, was the liaison agent for the district cadres in charge of the three villages of Hương Mỹ, Minh Đức, and Tân Trung, on the chance that I could find out where the province organization was located. Right that night I had to take the risk of rowing away in a sampan in the company of Mót, a fifteen year old boy. We crossed the Cổ Chiên river and entered the Bương Chạy estuary and then, at the risk to our own lives, went past the post near the Cầu Móng bridge. This was the most dangerous spot because the reactionaries here knew me. When I was near Mrs. Năm's house, it became light, so I had to sit in the rice fields and wait for it to get dark before going in to avoid detection. The moment I came in I told Ngoan to go and look for the cadres. He left immediately, carrying a lantern and pretending that he was going out to catch some fish. Late at night, Ngoan came back with comrade Sáu Huấn. Meeting the local "god of the soil" [e.g., someone very familiar with the local terrain and conditions] I was very happy and asked where the province leadership committee was located. He could not tell me much:

—Last night I met comrade Ba Đào, the head of the province office, in the company of Ba Cầu, a cadre from Mỏ Cày district, but I don't know where they are now.

When he heard that I had to urgently communicate a resolution from the higher levels to the province leadership committee, Sáu Huấn eagerly volunteered to go and look for them. I was very impatient and anxious and wanted to go with him, but since we had no idea where the others were, I had no choice but to stay behind at Mrs. Năm's house. I waited for one whole day before I could see comrades Ba Đào and Ba Cầu.

Fortunately comrade Hai Thủy, a member of the Standing Committee of the province also came. Seeing me, they immediately asked:

—What's the new policy?

I could not hide my enthusiasm:

—It's great!

But when I asked them about the province leadership committee, none of them knew where it was. Comrade Hai Thủy had been staying in this area to keep track of the task of proselytizing enemy troops. Ba Đào had been away on mission for a week and had not had any contact with the committee. I was mad with worry. There was no better solution, so I told them about the new resolution and asked for their opinion. I said:

—If we wait until we find the whole province leadership committee we will lose the opportunity. We represent only a minority of the committee here because only comrade Hai Thủy and I are members of the province leadership committee, so we can't take it upon ourselves to act right away. However, will we dare to take action and bear responsibility [toward the committee]?

When they heard me say this, the comrades sat silent and deep in thought. Normally when uprising and armed struggle were mentioned they would be full of ardor. Comrade Hai Thủy was a small, shriveled man, but he had served as the commander of the district unit during the nine year resistance and so was very familiar with military matters. Comrade Ba Đào was a village unit commander during the resistance and led his unit into battles many times, earning the reputation as a brave, fearless man. As for Ba Cầu and Sáu Huấn, they both loved military activities. Hai Thủy said:

—We definitely must act right away to be on schedule, and I think that after the uprising takes place we'll be able to reestablish contact.

We agreed unanimously. Right the next night—January 2, 1960—we held a formal conference to discuss in detail the goals, requirements, and concrete plans of action in Bến Tre province. To maintain secrecy, the meeting was not held in Mrs. Năm's room but was moved to the rice fields, and the tomb of landlord Nhơn was used as the conference site. This was the spot where tyrannical soldiers had lain in ambush and killed many of our comrades.

At 8:00 P.M., Ngoan led us to the conference site. We sat on top of the grave in the middle of a vast rice field. It was so dark we could not make out each other's face. Besides us, there were only the old man who was Mrs. Năm's husband and his three children— Hai Mới, Nam, and Ngoan standing guard around the rice field while pretending to fish. There were in all eight key cadres from the local area attending the conference.

The meeting was quiet but solemn, and the comrades and I felt very moved. I reported to the conference on what I knew of the enemy's situation and of our own situation, about the strong and weak points of the enemy, about the factors which were favorable to us, about our difficulties and the revolutionary capacity of the masses. I also reported on the new policy of the higher levels as well as the mission, goals, requirements, and forthcoming plan of action. During the discussion, most of the comrades were enthusiastic about the fact that the higher levels had allowed [political action] to be combined with armed struggle, but they wondered how the uprising could be carried out when we had no weapons. Once the uprising occurred and the enemy struck back, what would we rely on to defend ourselves? If we rose up but failed to hold our grounds, the enemy would terrorize us and an additional number of comrades operating clandestinely would be uncovered. What would we do then?

In the end, we unanimously decided to emulate the experience of the nine year resistance and of the August revolution which were brought to success by people who were barehanded. At present, there were many more factors in our favor [than during the resistance]: the masses understood the revolution and had acquired a definite level of consciousness, and their hatred of the enemy was very deep and intense. The ranks of the cadres were still thin, but they were firm and determined to destroy the enemy. The ranks of the enemy were rent with dissension and a number of them had links with the revolution. We were supported by a strong and reconstructed socialist North. I told the comrades:

—The main thing is for us to have confidence in the masses and to stay close to them to carry out the struggle. If we do this we'll achieve success.

All the comrades engaged in a lively and detailed discussion. To tell the truth, that was the first opportunity for them to express all the thoughts they had nurtured in their minds in these past few years. I had never been as fully aware of my heavy responsibility toward the future of the revolution and the lives of the people as I was at that moment. After the discussion was concluded, the conference unanimously decided to initiate a week-long drive to mobilize the entire population to rise up, annihilate the enemy and destroy their vise-like grip over the people, liberate the countryside, and become the masters of their rice fields and orchards. Strong areas would carry out intense struggles while weaker ones would do the best they could, and all areas should be prepared to come to each other's aid. The conference designated Cù Lao Minh island[18] which included the three districts of Minh Tân, Mỏ Cày, and Thạnh Phú, as the first area to rise up, with Mỏ Cày serving as the main focus. The uprising would take place from the night of January 17 to January 25th, 1960.

The conference discussed for a long time and in minute details how the uprising would be organized and carried out. First, we had to immediately set up action cells comprising cadres and unswervingly loyal sympathizers who would be armed with spears, to eliminate the traitors and tyrants. Youths from one village would be sent to another to operate, disguised as newly arrived Main Force units.[19] The conference hit upon the idea of producing a large quantity of various types of rifles made out of wood and coconut trunk, and to have many covers for rifles made, small ones and large ones, to give the impression that our armed forces were large and to frighten the enemy. Village officials, security police agents, and informers were divided into three categories: (a) tyrants who had blood debts toward the people, (b) those who were lukewarm in their service [to the Diệm regime], and (c) those who had been forced to serve. Landlords were also divided into three categories: (a) those who acted as henchmen for the enemy, or relied on the enemy to suppress the people, (b) those who were neutral, and (c) those who had children serving in the revolution. The action cells had to keep close watch over the tyrants who had incurred blood debts toward the people, so that once the masses rose up they could be nabbed immediately—otherwise if there was any delay these fellows would get away.

In the political field, we planned to set up a hard-core force which would operate openly under legal cover to mobilize the people over a wide area. We should lose no time in recruiting good people into revolutionary organizations so as to expand our military and political forces quickly and strongly in order to create conditions for continuous attacks and to achieve continuous success. We would make preparations to win over the soldiers' families and mobilize and motivate them—once the uprising started—to go into the posts and appeal to their husbands or sons to turn around and join the revolution. The most serious difficulty confronting us at this juncture was the shortage of cadres at a time when there were so many

---

[18] Bến Tre province has two islands: Cù Lao Minh and Cù Lao Bảo. *Footnote in text.* (This is the NLF administrative division of Bến Tre. *Trans.*)

[19] Main Force units are regular army units. This disguise was intended to create an impression of military strength. *Trans.*

tasks to attend to. So, we decided to recall all the *điều lắng*[20] cadres and to mobilize all the cadres in the province and district agencies and send them to the villages and hamlets to directly motivate the people. Finally, before parting we unanimously adopted the following slogans: (a) the attacks should be relentless, (b) once the movement was set in motion, it should be developed to its utmost capacity, without constraints, and (c) once the storm and wind started to blow, the boats should boldly hoist their sails and glide over the waves. (The intention here was to counteract hesitation and reluctance to boldly move forward.)

When it came to the division of labor, the comrades assigned me the task of keeping track of the overall movement. Comrades Thủy and Ba Đào were put in charge of military affairs, while Sáu Huấn and Ba Cầu returned to Minh Tân and Mỏ Cày to propagate the policy and then go down to the villages to directly lead the movement. Each of them would be in charge of from one to three villages.

The discussion drew to a close as the morning approached. We agreed to meet again on January 12, 1960 to review the preparations for the last time. I had not had any sleep for the last couple of nights but felt neither sleepy nor tired. In the night, we could hear Mrs. Năm's curses echoing from afar. She was still cursing those who betrayed the people and sold the country [to the foreigners]. The comrades dispersed and disappeared in the rice fields, while I returned to Mrs. Năm's house to meet the representative of Thạnh Phú district who had been unable to come on time [to attend the meeting]. The moment I got there, Mrs. Năm gave me rice gruel cooked in chicken broth to eat, a gesture which moved me deeply. It turned out that at the time she was cursing the enemy she was actually cooking rice gruel to feed the cadres. I had just sat down next to her when Ngoan told me that comrade Bảy Tranh wanted to see me immediately. I remembered that Tranh—a member of the Mỏ Cày District Party Committee during the resistance—had resigned because of ill health and I had not seen him for a long time. The moment he saw me he said right away:

— Sáu Huấn told me you're here. I've come to ask you to give me a task to perform—any task. The time for action is drawing close and everyone is busy as can be, but I'm just sitting idle with nothing to do and this makes me very sad.

Seeing that he was still as thin as a stick I comforted him:

—Don't worry about running out of things to do. There will always be something for you to do sooner or later, so just wait. The main thing for you is to recover your health completely.

He pleaded with me:

—If you don't want me to do anything too demanding, then give me something easy to do.

I suddenly thought of our policy to organize "fake" troops, so I gave him the

---

[20] Cadres who had been sent to operate underground in a local area. *Footnote in text.*

task of carving the insignia of the 502nd Battalion,[21] a famous unit in the Plain of Reeds which was greatly feared by the enemy, and assigned him the responsibility of guiding the implementation of the resolution in the two villages of An Định and Tân Trung. Bảy Tranh had just left when comrade Hai Chiến arrived. It was almost daylight. I went into Mrs. Năm's room to relay the resolution to Hai Chiến. Ngoan and his brother stood guard out on the road. Mrs. Năm was in the outer room and had stopped cursing. When she overheard me discuss ways to deal with the tyrannical landlords, she sneaked in and said:

—Brother and sister, allow me to contribute my opinion.

Comrade Hai Chiến told her:

—We respect you as much as our own parents, so don't address us like that.

She brushed him aside:

—I call you "brother" and "sister" because I respect the revolution, so just let me address you that way.

I had to interject because I was afraid that if she got mad and raised her voice, we would be detected:

—If you've an opinion to contribute, please tell us.

—Brother and sister, please don't let children of landlords join our ranks, all right? They're people who would surrender to you in the morning and betray you at night, and can't be trusted.

She turned around and left the room the moment she finished speaking. We turned our heads and followed her with our eyes, fully agreeing with her sharp idea. My discussion with Hai Chiến lasted until late afternoon. He was in complete agreement and only had the same general reservations which we also shared. However, that day he seemed to me a lot more quiet than usual. He had been operating with me for a long time. I had introduced him to his wife—Miss Tám—the widow of comrade Thanh who had been killed, so he and his wife were very close to me. Noting his quiet and reflective mood, I thought he was worried about his forthcoming mission and guessed that perhaps he had been tired out by the trip he had made to come here. I asked:

—Do you have any other questions?

—No, I only have a personal matter to tell you, and that is Tám has been arrested.

---

[21] This refers to a famous battalion of the religious sects operating in the Plain of Reeds which at that time had just won a major battle in Hồng Nghĩa district, Kiến Phong province. See Tô Minh Trung, "Ngọn cờ đầu," in *Nghiên Cứu Lịch Sử*, No. 118, January 1969, p. 49, and Tạ Xuân Linh, "Bến Tre," in *Vietnam Courier*, No. 27, August 1974, p. 7.*Trans.*

Before I could say anything to comfort him, he continued:

—This time around Tám will be liberated, I'm certain of that.

Having said this, he hurriedly got ready to leave. He pulled out his revolver, checked it, and then tucked it inside [his shirt] over his belly, looking as though he was about to give the enemy their just dessert.

* * *

During this period informers were everywhere keeping an eye on things, so we only indoctrinated a number of hard-core sympathizers and grassroot bases, usually referred to as the "steadfast and loyal masses" (*quần chúng chí cốt*) about our policy, but we did not tell them when the uprising would occur. In addition, we stimulated the hatred of the people and motivated them to wait for the day of action. Though we maintained absolute secrecy, the preparations among the people were very energetic and spirited. Boys and girls gathered in groups of three or five to practice martial arts. Forges worked day and night turning out machetes. In some areas people moved the forges into the forest to work. The carpenters produced [dummy] rifles, while the people were busy getting drums and wooden blocks ready.

The work was proceeding at a furious pace when we were struck by a dreadful news which hit us like a thunderbolt. It was January 14th. While I was in Bình Khánh village to check the situation and contribute my ideas to the leadership there, someone came and told me that Bảy Tranh had been captured by the soldiers. Comrade Bảy Tranh was the man who had met me in the middle of the night in Mrs. Năm's house and asked me to give him something to do, and I had assigned him the task of carving [the insignia of the 502nd Battalion on] rifle butts. He had made a few dozen and sent them to various areas. He knew all about the concerted uprising. If he could not bear the torture and confessed everything then the whole operation would be in jeopardy. I was even more worried when I heard about the circumstances of his arrest.

Comrade Tranh was arrested because he had tried to contact his wife who was not active in the revolution and lived in Ba Tri. They had been married a long time and had a few children. During his illness he occasionally sent news to his wife and asked her to come and visit him. This time, he asked an acquaintance to take a letter to her, in which he pretended to be a merchant arranging a meeting with her for a business transaction. The enemy in Ba Tri got hold of the letter and arrested her. They tortured her for a long time and in the end, unable to bear it any longer, she confessed that the letter was from her husband. They forced her to take them to the meeting place so they could capture Bảy Tranh. She struggled with herself for a long time and finally came to the naive conclusion that the designated site was probably just the place where she could contact him and not the place where he was living. She had no choice but to take the enemy there, hoping that he would run away when he found out that she was under arrest and would not wait for her. But contrary to her expectations she guided the enemy to capture her husband. They searched him and found a grenade he had procured for the day of the concerted uprising.

I was waiting for more news when Ngoan arrived in the middle of the day to give me another piece of bad news:

—I had just returned from studying documents on the Youth Group and had just lay down to sleep when someone tapped my feet and told me to get up. It was brother Sáu Huấn who told me to go to Tân Trung to find out whether it's true that sister Tư Lực had been arrested.

I panicked and asked Ngoan:

—Is she the liaison agent for the district?

—Yes.

Ngoan had just left when another person came to inform me:

—[Tư] Lực had just led the enemy to Mrs. Năm's house to arrest you. When they arrived at the gate, they ran into Nam, Ngoan's brother. Lực pointed him out to the enemy but he escaped. They then went into the house and arrested Miss Hai, Mrs. Năm's daughter whose husband regrouped to the North. Mrs. Năm held her tight and wouldn't let go of her, but she couldn't fight them off so she cursed them.

That was on the 15th of January. The concerted uprising was scheduled to take place in two days' time. If Bảy Tranh and Tư Lực confessed, the enemy would be on guard and we would run into a lot of difficulties. At that time, comrade Hai Thủy who was stationed in the area further north was making preparations to destroy the post in Định Thủy village which was the locality slated to rise up first. The situation was extremely critical. I wanted to go and see comrade Hai Thủy immediately to discuss a plan to deal with all eventualities, but to go from Bình Khánh to Định Thủy I would have to pass by many dangerous enemy posts. I had to take the risk of making the trip in the company of Mrs. Hai, a very reliable sympathizer. She was about sixty years old. The two of us ferried a sampan, pretending to be traders, going through Mỏ Cày district town and then past the Định Thủy post to meet comrade Hai Thủy on January 16th. When she got home, Mrs. Hai was arrested by the enemy who tortured her savagely, but she maintained her spirit as Bảy Tranh had done and refused to divulge anything. This was why the enemy was unable to find out anything.

During those last couple of days [before the uprising] Hai Thủy and I felt very nervous and anxious. Each day seemed to pass by so slowly. On the morning of January 17th, the atmosphere everywhere was busy and festive. Comrade Hai Thủy said:

—If nothing happens this morning, we should go ahead.

I agreed because I was afraid that the longer we delayed the more likely our plan would be discovered. Hai Thủy kept me in Định Thủy to reinforce the leadership of the test site and to keep track of the overall situation.

January 17, 1960 was a day full of hope and worry for the patriotic people in Bến Tre province. I waited for the attack on the canton militia unit, composed of two squads stationed in Định Thủy village, to occur. The comrades had decided to attack while the militiamen were sleeping and off their guards. At the appointed time, a hard-core youth who knew the militia commander entered in a panic to look for him concerning an urgent matter. This fellow was still awake while his troops were sound asleep. Our forces, disguised as ordinary merchants, lay in ambush around the communal house. Being suspicious by nature, the commander pulled out his Sten pistol and came to the door of the communal house. His arms akimbo, he tilted his bearded chin and asked haughtily:

—What's the matter?

Our comrade obsequiously bent down to whisper in his ear, as though to transmit something important, then suddenly raised his arm and hit him hard on the nape of the neck. He collapsed right away. Our forces poured in and called on the troops to surrender. A number of them bolted and fled in disorder, while the rest surrendered. We captured enough weapons to equip about a squad of men. The Định Thủy post was only about one kilometer from here. Hai Thủy was afraid that the soldiers belonging to the unit of the canton militia commander would go and warn the post which would then take precautions, so he ordered the immediate capture of the post at 3:00 P.M. There were sympathizers among the soldiers in this post, and before the news [of the attack on the militia unit] reached the post, our infiltrators rose up and burned it down. The flames billowed high in the sky. The brothers brought back about ten additional rifles.

We let a number of soldiers flee to Mỏ Cày district town to report that Việt Cộng troops had come to take Định Thủy post and were on their way to Mỏ Cày in large numbers. As we had suspected, the enemy in Mỏ Cày just fired a few artillery rounds and stayed put in their post, not daring to send out reinforcements. Our first attack was successful and we had seized a large number of weapons. We were greatly encouraged and were even more determined to smash the vise-like grip of the enemy. I discussed with comrade Hai Thủy about sending two rifles each to Thạnh Phú and Minh Tân districts to use as "capital" and relaying the news of victory in Mỏ Cày to the comrades so they could emulate us. The rest of the weapons were handed over to Hai Thủy and Ba Đào to replace the wooden rifles, since the "502nd Battalion" at that time only had two muskets and one Carbine with a broken butt.

At dusk that day, comrade Hai Thủy and I led the troops from Định Thủy to reinforce the villages of Phước Hiệp and Bình Khánh. Định Thủy was the only area that acted early, and Thạnh Phú, Minh Tân, and Mỏ Cày would rise up in concert that night which would belong to us. The roads reverberated with the thudding footsteps of our own people. I remembered the nights when I had to feel my way in the rice fields, hitting my head against coconut trees, bumping my chest against the embankments, getting chilled to the marrows—yet I kept on going, wading all night. I felt very proud and honored that I had survived to be present on the day when the revolution erupted. My happiness increased when I thought that tonight our people's aspirations would be satisfied.

Sometime after 9:00 P.M., I had just arrived in the permanent office when I heard the sounds of drums and wooden blocks echoing from one village to another and resounding everywhere, followed by the happy shouts of the people:

—Friends, it's begun!

—It's the death knell for Diệm!

As the night advanced, the sound of drums and wooden bells intensified and became insistent as though urging everyone to rise up. This was the people's signal for combat being transmitted everywhere. The drums, wooden blocks, rope, and sticks that the enemy had forced the villagers to have on hand to capture patriots were now being used by the people to tie up those who had sold the country. Suddenly there was a shout:

—The post is on fire, and it's burning rapidly!

The forces encircling the posts had been ordered to burn down any posts they captured. The people immediately tore up the flags and burned the plaques bearing their house numbers and their family registers.[22] On the roads, the villagers cut down trees to erect barriers and block the movement of the enemy. On both banks of the river where communication trenches and barbed wire crisscrossed in a tangled maze, boats stopped to listen to our propaganda. All the posts were surrounded by the people who made appeals to the soldiers through bullhorns. Once in a while, "a heavy gun" exploded (actually bamboo sections filled with acetylene). It was a night of terrifying thunder and lightning striking the enemy on the heads. Attacked by surprise, they were scared out of their wits and stayed put in the posts. Occasionally explosive charges exploded, sounding like mortars or grenade launchers. The people who had the most difficult task tonight were the units in charge of eliminating tyrannical local officials and agents—the core of the machinery of control in the hamlets and villages. Each member had to disguise himself with mask and change his clothing in order to prevent the enemy from recognizing him. Only a few comrades appeared publicly to mobilize the people and act as their representatives to condemn this group [e.g., the officials and agents]. At 5:00 A.M., we sent for the comrade in charge of the elimination of tyrants in the closest village to review the results. Carrying a machete, he came to report:

—Everything's been done. The local officials and agents all lost their customary arrogance and became humble. When we rushed in and shouted to them, only one reactionary fled, the rest surrendered right away. They were all shaking and trembling.

This comrade who was of average height was wearing a very neat Western suit and a felt hat, and carried a machete which made "him" look very tough. "His" voice was, however, very soft. I thought it sounded like a girl's voice, the voice of someone I knew. I asked:

—Are you Miss Thu's brother?

—This is Thu herself!

---

[22] These were administrative devices used by the government of Ngô Đình Diệm to ensure better control of the population. *Trans.*

Then she burst our laughing and said:

—I followed the decision to disguise myself to deceive the enemy and also to put the minds of the men in my cell at ease. They despise us women, you know.

I also burst out laughing. Accompanying Thu was a skinny and short boy, about fifteen to seventeen years old, who was carrying a machete almost as big as himself. Thu said:

—That's little Kim! When we arrested Đốp, the tyrannical landlord, Kim jumped in and tied him up. He only wants to join the revolution and doesn't want to go back to his life as a servant for the landlord.

I congratulated Kim:

—You're very brave. Do you want to join the army?

He blurted out:

—If you had let me kill him I would have done so right away. I hate him a lot!

As the situation evolved successfully, the leadership of the committee of the Concerted Uprising right that night drafted a military order which was then posted everywhere in the areas under the temporary control of the enemy to heighten the prestige of the revolution. The contents of the military order included the following points:

—All soldiers, no matter how serious their crimes were, if they repented and rejoined the ranks of the people with their weapons, would be forgiven.

—Village and hamlet officials, heads of inter-family groups, security policemen, and informers who resigned and surrendered to the people would be forgiven by the people.

—Landlords who had relied on the power of the enemy to seize the land of the peasants and increase their rents should return what they had taken to the peasants.

This military order would remain in force from January 17 to 25, 1960. Anyone who disobeyed it would be condemned to death by the people and had their properties confiscated. This order was written in large letters and posted in strategic areas and in the towns.

In the first night of the concerted uprising, the enemy's machinery of control in a number of villages crumbled. In some villages, the officials went to hand in their resignations even before our arrival. The villagers then forced them to issue the order to have the flags torn and family registers burned.[23] The reactionaries with

---

[23] Lists of family members that Ngô Đình Diệm had forced the people to declare. *Footnote in text.*

blood debts and the tyrannical landlords whom we had not managed to capture fled. The people became the complete masters of a number of hamlets and villages. Our task on January 18th and the following days was to track down and arrest the remaining tyrants, besiege the posts, take over the remaining hamlets and villages, destroy the roads, cut down trees to build roadblocks, and get ready to fight if the enemy brought in troops to attack us. We organized meetings of peasants to discuss the equal distribution of the rice fields we had seized. The people were extremely encouraged. At dawn on January 18th, I went to the road to check how the work of sabotage was progressing and to take a look at the situation. Suddenly I heard aircraft noise coming from the direction of Mỏ Cày. The people shouted:

—A helicopter is landing in Mỏ Cày!

I guessed that some "big shot" was coming to devise ways to thwart our work. The aircraft landed and stayed for fifteen minutes and then grunted upward. In the afternoon, we heard that the Bến Tre province authorities had sent a helicopter to evacuate the district chief of Mỏ Cày. There was no riposte from the enemy during the whole day of January 18th. In the night of January 18th and in the early morning of January 19th, the villages held a rally to display the strength and ardor of the people. The villagers felt very satisfied, especially when the policemen, tyrants, officials, spies, and landlords with blood debts were led out to be executed in front of the people. Every one of them was guilty of countless crimes and deserved the death sentence. However, in accordance with the lenient policy of the revolution, only the gang leaders—the most cruel and treacherous of them all—were executed. The others, those who had blood debts but confessed their crimes and acknowledged their guilt, were only given a suspended death sentence. They were ordered to move to the district and province towns to live in repentance, and if any of them committed new crimes they would be executed.

That whole week, the enemy stayed put in their positions. They trembled before the power and prestige of the revolution. Since we had eliminated their machinery of control in the villages—their eyes and arms—they had no way of knowing what the real situation was. Two days after Định Thủy and Bình Khánh posts fell, the enemy abandoned Phước Hiệp post and fled. These three villages were completely liberated. On January 19th, Mỏ Cày district dispatched a column of troops to Định Thủy post to check the situation. Forewarned, comrade Hai Thủy organized a "trick" ambush—complete with crisscrossing communication trenches, foxholes, mortars, submachine gun and machine gun emplacements, and positioned a cell to fire on landing crafts. When the clash occurred, the moment we opened fire the soldiers fled toward Mỏ Cày and then sent reconnaissance agents back to check. Seeing the grandiose defense network, they became frightened and reported to their superiors:

—It's true that large units are involved. It's true that liberation forces from the North have arrived!

Emboldened, the villagers stepped up their efforts to eliminate village officials and tyrants, surround the posts, called on the soldiers to surrender, and seized weapons. In some places, whenever the soldiers manning the posts wanted to go to the latrine or to fetch fresh water, they had to ask permission from the guerrillas, otherwise if they took the liberty of doing so without asking they would be shot at by the guerrillas—this was the same tactic of sniping that had been employed at Điện Biên Phủ. A week after the concerted uprising began, we reviewed the results and found that we had captured about ten posts and that the apparatus of control which the enemy had spent six years consolidating had either been shaken to the foundations or had disintegrated. The enemy, however, remained completely ignorant of our strength, as though they were deaf and blind.

* * *

We captured almost one hundred weapons. The leadership committee had a heated debate on how many units should be formed. Some wanted to set up a battalion, some wanted a company, others wanted to keep our old troop strength of two platoons. Comrade Đào who had been put in command of the troops seemed to want a large force:

—The youths are extremely eager to join the troops. Even if we had a thousand rifles at our disposal we would have no difficulty finding enough men to handle them.

I agreed with the idea of setting up a company sized unit. I thought this was a reasonable size, and the main idea was to choose and arm the most committed and most loyal to the revolution. Those who did not have any firearms would continue to carry machetes and sticks, and would be fully equipped gradually. I also proposed that a campaign to "tackle the soldiers and seize their weapons" be initiated among the youths; and anyone who could get his hands on a rifle in this manner would have the priority of keeping his weapon. Because of this, young boys and girls were very eager to practice martial arts in the hope of "tackling" the soldiers and taking their weapons in order to be able to join the armed forces. During a trip I made to An Định village, two young men came to see me and pleaded with me to let them join the troops so they could avenge the deaths of their family members who had been murdered by the Americans and Diệm. They met all the criteria, but they had not managed to seize any weapons. The Cầu Sập post was still standing in An Định village so I proposed to them:

—You still have a legal status, why not try to "tackle" the soldiers at Cầu Sập, take their weapons, and join the troops?

They promised [to do this] and then left immediately. There was a large rice mill near Cầu Sập, and the soldiers guarding the bridge used to sneak down to the mill to tease the girls there. The two youths contacted an old woman in the mill who organized a game and called all the girls, the two young men and two soldiers into the mill to have a "weighing" contest and see who weighed the most. One soldier climbed on the scale carrying his rifle, but the old lady shouted:

—You must remove your rifle and ammunition, this way we'll know what your real weight is.

He thought she was serious and did as told. The first soldier had not finished weighing when the second one hastily removed his rifle and ammunition, took off his shirt, and grinning with pride displayed his large chest to the girls. The golden opportunity had arrived. The youths jumped in, pinned the soldiers down, and beat them till they passed out, seized a carbine and a Sten pistol, and fled. The moment they got home they immediately sent me a letter with the news: "Even if you want us to stay here and work now [we won't listen], we're determined to join the troops and don't want to stay home any longer. We're anxiously waiting for you to call us, and the moment you call we'll join the army."

Mrs. Năm (in Minh Đức) also sent us a message asking us to accept Ngoan and his brother into the army. They both were very eager to go and fight the enemy! Even if she had to stay by herself, she would be able to manage. In fact, usually once backbone elements like her children and the two youths in An Định became conscious of their mission to fight the enemy, their parents were unable to stop them [from joining up]. Little Kim whom Miss Thu had introduced to me was accepted right away into the liberation army. Since we did not have enough weapons, he agreed to carry a machete almost as big as himself. He was an orphan, his entire family, who had worked as servants for landlords from generation to generation, having all died before. His unit now became his beloved family.

The first unit of Bến Tre province, born in the concerted uprising and growing continuously, was composed entirely of hardcore youths who harbored a deep hatred for the enemy and for this reason fought very bravely. The first liberation platoon was presented to the people at an inauguration ceremony in a coconut grove in Bình Khánh village, Mỏ Cày district.

* * *

About ten days later the enemy began to recover their wits. Mỏ Cày district town and a number of posts were still intact. The enemy finally realized that we had risen up with bare hands and that no 502nd Battalion, no South Vietnam or North Vietnam Liberation Forces had come to our assistance. But by the time they discovered this it had become too late. Their government apparatus in the countryside and their frightening grip over the villages and hamlets had been broken. They immediately sent a large column to push into Bình Khánh and Phước Hiệp villages, but each time they came they suffered some losses.

On February 22, 1960 they sent a company from Mỏ Cày to attack Phước Hiệp. We set up an ambush with over a platoon of men and destroyed one of their platoons, seized two submachine guns, two semiautomatic rifles, and ten Mas rifles. They were determined to deploy all their strength and retaliate against us. Around February 24th, they focused their attack on Phước Hiệp, Bình Khánh, and Định Thủy, the three villages that had risen up with great force during the concerted uprising in Mỏ Cày district. They assembled about thirteen thousand soldiers who pushed their way in from Sài Gòn, Trà Vinh, and Bến Tre province town. Their propaganda said that they would annihilate us and restore order. Seeing the large enemy force, the villagers became worried and demoralized. We were also caught in the enemy encirclement, but our policy specified that the cadres should not abandon the people and should stay at all costs to resist the sweep operation, maintain the movement, and prevent it from collapsing. Comrades Hai Thủy and Ba

Đào were in charge of keeping track of the enemy's movements, selecting the weakest of their columns, and waiting until nightfall to destroy it to break the back of the operation. The soldiers angrily searched everywhere without finding our forces. Meanwhile, wherever they went they were wounded by the "sky horse" rifles (*ngựa trời*). At 5:00 P.M. on February 25th, comrade Thủy led an attack on a company size column and after fifteen minutes of fighting destroyed about two platoons. In their fright and confusion the enemy shot each other, killing an additional number. Taking advantage of the darkness, we withdrew safely, losing only one comrade who was killed by a stray bullet.

The "sky horse" rifle appeared for the first time in this battle. This was an invention by a guerrilla who devised it from the principle of explosives, used in producing land mines. The barrel of the rifle consisted of a long steel pipe. The rifle had legs like a mortar and was detonated when a wire was pulled as in the case of mines. The charge consisted of explosives mixed with steel pellets and glass shards dipped in urine and snake poison. The firing range was ten meters, and anyone who was hit—even if it was just a scratch on the skin—would die right away. The masses spread the rumor that this was a new weapon, and whenever they heard the "sky horse" mentioned, the enemy soldiers fled in disorder.

While the enemy was concentrating their forces to surround us, the leadership committee had each area spread the news that we were about to attack Mỏ Cày district town and Bến Tre province town. At the same time we had the people prepare sampans and get ready to supply rice to large units. As expected, the enemy heard the news the next day. They gave up the operation, and withdrew their forces in a panic to defend these towns. In this operation, seeing that our losses had been insignificant while the enemy had lost over one hundred men, the people felt very encouraged. The women capitalized on this situation to work on the soldiers, and a large number of them deserted. Small children picked up and delivered to us thousands of cartridges belonging to the enemy. However, the reactionary enemy left behind a force to occupy Phước Hiệp in the hope of intimidating the people and of gradually encroaching on our territory and then taking it back. Most of these troops were Catholics and they were extremely brutal and reactionary. Within ten days, they arrested twenty youths, liquidated them, and buried them around the post. They conscripted the villagers to do forced labor, building the road from Phước Hiệp to Bình Khánh, and terrorized the people in an extremely brutal manner.

The villagers' ardor declined noticeably. The comrades in the village pleaded with us to send armed units down to destroy the post. We also wanted to destroy this gang badly and relieve our anger, but our armed forces were still weak. So we discussed ways to put a stop to the enemy's killing while still maintaining the initiative and the legal status of the masses. Everyone unanimously agreed that we should organize immediately a large group of women who would push their way into Mỏ Cày district town to denounce the crimes of the soldiers in Phước Hiệp.

The first time, over five thousand women—including old women, young girls, and children—from the villages of Phước Hiệp, Bình Khánh, Định Thủy, Đa Phước Hội, An Định, and Thành Thới, formed a huge force, wearing mourning bands and ragged clothes and carrying their children, and surged into Mỏ Cày district town. They demanded an end to terrorism and compensation for the deaths caused by the soldiers, and punishment of the brutes in Phước Hiệp village. The district chief was scared out of his mind and shouted to the soldiers to shut the gates tightly and not to allow anyone to enter. The people stayed in front of the district headquarters, defecating and urinating on the spot, and refused to go home. Among the women was an eighteen year old girl who had been blind since childhood but was very enthusiastic about struggling against the enemy. A policeman teased her:

—This blind girl can't see anything, and what does she feel she can accomplish by joining the struggle?

She retorted right away:

—I'm blind but I know enough to follow the path of light, and this is much better than you people who can see but are following a blind road.

The policeman did not know what to say. The women praised her:

—She's blind but she's enlightened.

The girl was also a good singer. During the struggle she sang guerrilla songs which left the soldiers reflective and less arrogant. The tug of war lasted for five days and five nights, and each day the group was reinforced with more women coming to lend a hand, and the struggle became more inflamed. In the end, the district chief had to open the gate and come out to accept the demands of the people, agreeing to withdraw all the soldiers from Phước Hiệp village. At the height of the "concerted uprising" in Bến Tre province, the successful struggle of the women in Mỏ Cày district on March 15, 1960 initiated a new form of struggle by the masses which proved to be very effective. The Americans and Diệm were very afraid of this powerful force [constituted by the women] and gave it a special name: the long-haired troops.

XI

At the beginning of April 1960, we held a meeting to make a preliminary review of the success of the concerted uprising in the districts of Cù Lao Minh island and to draw experiences for timely contribution to the uprising which was scheduled to take place all over Bến Tre province. Our experiences were very rich but our level of understanding was low so we failed to bring out the best experiences of the masses. Later, the higher levels reviewed our experiences and deduced the policy of attacking the enemy on "two legs" (*hai chân*) and with "three prongs" (*ba mũi giáp công*).[24] I was very pleased with this policy and proceeded to apply it to mobilize the movement and spread it to every area.

During the conference, the collective [leadership] gave me a key role in the leadership committee of Bến Tre province. I was very encouraged by the new responsibility but was worried that my limited capacity would prevent me from completing my mission. At first, I declined the responsibility, but the collective

---

[24] The "two legs" are military action and political action. The three prongs are: *chính trị* (political action), *quân sự* (military action), and *binh vận* (proselytizing enemy soldiers). *Trans.*

[leadership] passed a resolution and I was forced to go along. The comrades told me:

—The women's movement is very strong now, and they have the capacity to attack the enemy on all three fronts. You deserve to represent them. Don't be timid in your work, the collective [leadership] will help you and things will go smoothly.

In the ensuing phase of the "concerted uprising" which erupted in the few remaining districts, I was assigned the task of keeping close track of and giving guidance to Giồng Trôm district, the focus point (*điểm*) of the province. We held an all-night meeting and as morning broke I had to leave immediately to attend a meeting of district and village cadres. The key leaders of Giồng Trôm district, such as comrades Bê and Khác, were very eager to surpass Mỏ Cày district. But on this occasion, Giồng Trôm district did not enjoy the factor of surprise. The enemy had taken precautionary measures, but we attacked by ruse and were better at it than before. The task of proselytizing enemy soldiers proceeded apace. The political struggles in Giồng Trôm district taught us a new lesson: in order to achieve results, women should attack the enemy with sharp arguments while liberation troops were attacking them with weapons. The force taking part in the [political] struggle in Giồng Trôm district was twice as large as the one participating in the struggle in Mỏ Cày district previously. For the first time, we hoisted a vast array of banners and slogans, including those demanding the resignation of Ngô Đình Diệm and the dissolution of the puppet "National Assembly."

Just a few days after the uprising started, six villages in Giồng Trôm district were liberated and one hundred weapons were seized. In each village, from one hundred to three hundred people joined the group taking part in the face-to-face political struggle against the enemy. Within a short time, the wave of "concerted uprising" spread from Cù Lao Minh island to Cù Lao Bảo island, and broke out all over Bến Tre province. Vigorous movements developed in each and every province in the South. The majority of villages passed into the hands of the masses who became masters [of the countryside].

The people of Bến Tre province who had endured untold miseries during the past six years could now laugh, sing, and live. A new spirit was burning all over the countryside. The political forces held animated discussions about the struggle. Carpenters and blacksmiths raced to produce knives and machetes to kill the enemy. The workshops improved the sky-horse rifles, making them more lethal, and produced a batch of new weapons called "*mút nhét*" (primed rifles). At this time, the armed forces of the province were over one company in strength and each district had from one to two squads. Each village had from one to three rifles, but the majority of these were French muskets. Young girls stayed up many nights to sew "Main Force" green uniforms for the troops. An information office was set up in each hamlet in Giồng Trôm, Mỏ Cày, and Châu Thành districts. On each side of the road, slogans were drawn on tree trunks and caught everyone's eyes. On some days people from the province town came by the hundreds to visit the liberated areas.

After the gigantic foray of a fifteen thousand strong political force into Bến Tre province town, the Bến Tre province Committee of the National Front for the Liberation of South Vietnam was officially presented to the people. The creation of the Front was of vital significance for its aim was to consolidate the people's right to be masters of the countryside. While the high point of the concerted uprising was rising like a tidal wave sweeping everything in its path, the people became more insistent in their demand that the revolution set up an official organization to represent the strength, unity, and fighting force of the people, which would continue to lead the people to advance forward toward new successes in the resistance to save the country and oppose the American imperialist invaders and their henchmen— Ngô Đình Diệm and the gang of traitors. This was why the "National Front for the Liberation of South Vietnam"—the sole organization leading the resistance by the entire population of the South—was timely created and presented to the people on December 20, 1960.

Aware of this spirit, we made urgent preparations in order to present the Bến Tre province Liberation Front Committee to the people on December 26, 1960, that is to say six days after the birth of the National Front for the Liberation of South Vietnam. We decided to make it a big occasion by convoking a conference which would be attended by representatives of every population stratum in order to set up the Province Liberation Front Committee, and organizing a ceremony for about ten thousand people representing the countryside, the urban areas, all the religious groups, and the families of soldiers. We selected Mỹ Chánh, located less than five kilometers from Ba Tri district town, as the site for the presentation ceremony. The population here was large and the village was located in a favorable strategic terrain and had a big market, the Bến Bào market.

At dusk on December 26th, the rally began. We had electric lights and microphones which had been sent by workers in the province town as their contribution to the rally. Seeing the flag being hoisted which brightened up a whole section of the sky, we all felt very moved. So much blood shed by the comrades and people had dyed this glorious and eternal flag.

The Liberation Front Committee comprised fifteen people who represented every social strata, religious group, and political party. The committee solemnly appeared in front of the people and each member gave a speech. Mr. Ngợi, the representative of the Cao Đài Tiên Thiên sect, Mr. Hồ Háo Nghĩa, representing university and high school students, Mr. Ngôi, representing the national bourgeoisie, Mrs. Mười Quới, representing the women, brother Ba, representing the peasants—they all condemned the crimes of the enemy and expressed their gratitude toward and their confidence in the revolution, and pledged to unite and fight to the end to overthrow the Americans and Diệm.

I had the honor of representing the People's Revolutionary Party[25] and the Front, and on their behalf I made promises and pledges, and called on the people to propel the fight strongly forward. When I stepped down from the podium, many women embraced me and inquired after me with great concern. An old lady grasped my hand and wept:

—I'm Bích's aunt. Heavens, if he were still alive today he would be so happy seeing this scene.

Heavens! We embraced each other in happiness and sorrow. I was very moved and told her:

---

[25] This is the Southern branch of the Lao Động (workers) party. *Trans*

—Besides Bích, both my parents have been killed. I don't have anyone left, but there are so many other mothers and fathers who love me even more than their own children.

Talking about Bích in this place where he was born, I thought that this ceremony, by evoking an old memory, had taken on an added significance for me. I felt greatly cheered and asked my husband's aunt:

—If the enemy comes tomorrow and asks what you're doing here tonight, what will you say?

She replied without hesitating:

—What do you think I'll say? I'll say that the Front was born, that liberation troops and people attended in great numbers, in the tens of thousands. I wasn't afraid of them before, so why should I be afraid of them now that our forces are as strong as this?

I looked at the large popular force and felt overjoyed. The armed units had expanded rapidly. Bến Tre province now had close to a battalion of adequately armed troops. This was a real battalion, not a "fake" one. As for the strong and large "long haired" force, I did not even how how many battalions of them there were. From now on, on the road of resisting the Americans and their lackeys, our people would stand firm on the two powerful legs of military and political strength to fight and achieve victory. There was no other road to take.

In the face of this enormous and imposing force of the people, I felt very small, but I was full of self-confidence, like a small tree standing in a vast and ancient forest. In struggling against the enemy, I had come to fully realize that we had to have the strength of the whole forest in order to be able to stay the force of the strong winds and storms. As I thought about the protection and support of the people, about the enormous efforts that the revolution had expanded in educating and nurturing me, about the countless comrades and beloved peoples—some of whom I had mentioned but whose names I could never exhaustively enumerate—I felt more intimately bound, more so than ever before, to the road I had taken and had pledged to follow until my last days. This was the road for which I would sacrifice everything for the future of the revolution and for the interests of the masses. For me there was no other road to take.

After the ceremony broke up, I walked among the troops, carrying my knapsack. A few shots echoed from an enemy post nearby. A fighter joked:

—Hey, they're firing to salute the birth of the Front!

Another one immediately brushed his remark aside:

—Saluting like that isn't adequate. One of these days we'll have to go to the post and force them to kneel down to greet the Front and to surrender!

Everyone burst out laughing. We made our way leisurely on the large road, talking noisily as we walked under the sky of liberation full of stars and cooled by a strong breeze. And from all four directions of the island I could hear the rifle shots of the guerillas encircling and destroying the posts, as though urging everyone to quickly rush forward and eliminate the Americans and Diệm to liberate the South, so that the people of the whole country could soon be reunited under the spring sky of our native land full of the sweet fragrance of the milk fruit.

November 1965.

SOUTHEAST ASIA PROGRAM PUBLICATIONS
Cornell University

Studies on Southeast Asia

Number 42   *Thailand: The Politics of Despotic Paternalism* (revised edition), Thak
Chaloemtiarana. 2007. 284 pp. ISBN 0-8772-7742-7 (pb).

Number 41   *Two Views of Seventeenth-Century Vietnam: Christoforo Borri on
Cochinchina and Samuel Baron on Tonkin*, ed. Olga Dror and
K. W. Taylor. 2006. 290 pp. ISBN 0-8772-7741-9 (pb).

Number 40   *Laskar Jihad: Islam, Militancy, and the Quest for Identity in Post-New Order
Indonesia*, Noorhaidi Hasan. 2006. 266 pp. ISBN 0-877277-40-0 (pb).

Number 39   *The Indonesian Supreme Court: A Study of Institutional Collapse*,
Sebastiaan Pompe. 2005. 494 pp. ISBN 0-877277-38-9 (pb).

Number 38   *Spirited Politics: Religion and Public Life in Contemporary Southeast Asia*,
ed. Andrew C. Willford and Kenneth M. George. 2005. 210 pp.
ISBN 0-87727-737-0.

Number 37   *Sumatran Sultanate and Colonial State: Jambi and the Rise of Dutch
Imperialism, 1830-1907*, Elsbeth Locher-Scholten, trans. Beverley
Jackson. 2004. 332 pp. ISBN 0-87727-736-2.

Number 36   *Southeast Asia over Three Generations: Essays Presented to Benedict R. O'G.
Anderson*, ed. James T. Siegel and Audrey R. Kahin. 2003. 398 pp. ISBN
0-87727-735-4.

Number 35   *Nationalism and Revolution in Indonesia*, George McTurnan Kahin, intro.
Benedict R. O'G. Anderson (reprinted from 1952 edition, Cornell
University Press, with permission). 2003. 530 pp. ISBN 0-87727-734-6.

Number 34   *Golddiggers, Farmers, and Traders in the "Chinese Districts" of West
Kalimantan, Indonesia*, Mary Somers Heidhues. 2003. 316 pp.
ISBN 0-87727-733-8.

Number 33   *Opusculum de Sectis apud Sinenses et Tunkinenses (A Small Treatise on the
Sects among the Chinese and Tonkinese): A Study of Religion in China and
North Vietnam in the Eighteenth Century*, Father Adriano de St. Thecla,
trans. Olga Dror, with Mariya Berezovska. 2002. 363 pp.
ISBN 0-87727-732-X.

Number 32   *Fear and Sanctuary: Burmese Refugees in Thailand*, Hazel J. Lang. 2002.
204 pp. ISBN 0-87727-731-1.

Number 31   *Modern Dreams: An Inquiry into Power, Cultural Production, and the
Cityscape in Contemporary Urban Penang, Malaysia*, Beng-Lan Goh. 2002.
225 pp. ISBN 0-87727-730-3.

Number 30   *Violence and the State in Suharto's Indonesia*, ed. Benedict R. O'G.
Anderson. 2001. Second printing, 2002. 247 pp. ISBN 0-87727-729-X.

Number 29   *Studies in Southeast Asian Art: Essays in Honor of Stanley J. O'Connor*, ed.
Nora A. Taylor. 2000. 243 pp. Illustrations. ISBN 0-87727-728-1.

Number 28   *The Hadrami Awakening: Community and Identity in the Netherlands East
Indies, 1900-1942*, Natalie Mobini-Kesheh. 1999. 174 pp.
ISBN 0-87727-727-3.

Number 27   *Tales from Djakarta: Caricatures of Circumstances and their Human Beings*,
Pramoedya Ananta Toer. 1999. 145 pp. ISBN 0-87727-726-5.

Number 26 *History, Culture, and Region in Southeast Asian Perspectives*, rev. ed., O. W. Wolters. 1999. Second printing, 2004. 275 pp. ISBN 0-87727-725-7.

Number 25 *Figures of Criminality in Indonesia, the Philippines, and Colonial Vietnam*, ed. Vicente L. Rafael. 1999. 259 pp. ISBN 0-87727-724-9.

Number 24 *Paths to Conflagration: Fifty Years of Diplomacy and Warfare in Laos, Thailand, and Vietnam, 1778-1828*, Mayoury Ngaosyvathn and Pheuiphanh Ngaosyvathn. 1998. 268 pp. ISBN 0-87727-723-0.

Number 23 *Nguyễn Cochinchina: Southern Vietnam in the Seventeenth and Eighteenth Centuries*, Li Tana. 1998. Second printing, 2002. 194 pp. ISBN 0-87727-722-2.

Number 22 *Young Heroes: The Indonesian Family in Politics*, Saya S. Shiraishi. 1997. 183 pp. ISBN 0-87727-721-4.

Number 21 *Interpreting Development: Capitalism, Democracy, and the Middle Class in Thailand*, John Girling. 1996. 95 pp. ISBN 0-87727-720-6.

Number 20 *Making Indonesia*, ed. Daniel S. Lev, Ruth McVey. 1996. 201 pp. ISBN 0-87727-719-2.

Number 19 *Essays into Vietnamese Pasts*, ed. K. W. Taylor, John K. Whitmore. 1995. 288 pp. ISBN 0-87727-718-4.

Number 18 *In the Land of Lady White Blood: Southern Thailand and the Meaning of History*, Lorraine M. Gesick. 1995. 106 pp. ISBN 0-87727-717-6.

Number 17 *The Vernacular Press and the Emergence of Modern Indonesian Consciousness*, Ahmat Adam. 1995. 220 pp. ISBN 0-87727-716-8.

Number 16 *The Nan Chronicle*, trans., ed. David K. Wyatt. 1994. 158 pp. ISBN 0-87727-715-X.

Number 15 *Selective Judicial Competence: The Cirebon-Priangan Legal Administration, 1680–1792*, Mason C. Hoadley. 1994. 185 pp. ISBN 0-87727-714-1.

Number 14 *Sjahrir: Politics and Exile in Indonesia*, Rudolf Mrázek. 1994. 536 pp. ISBN 0-87727-713-3.

Number 13 *Fair Land Sarawak: Some Recollections of an Expatriate Officer*, Alastair Morrison. 1993. 196 pp. ISBN 0-87727-712-5.

Number 12 *Fields from the Sea: Chinese Junk Trade with Siam during the Late Eighteenth and Early Nineteenth Centuries*, Jennifer Cushman. 1993. 206 pp. ISBN 0-87727-711-7.

Number 11 *Money, Markets, and Trade in Early Southeast Asia: The Development of Indigenous Monetary Systems to AD 1400*, Robert S. Wicks. 1992. 2nd printing 1996. 354 pp., 78 tables, illus., maps. ISBN 0-87727-710-9.

Number 10 *Tai Ahoms and the Stars: Three Ritual Texts to Ward Off Danger*, trans., ed. B. J. Terwiel, Ranoo Wichasin. 1992. 170 pp. ISBN 0-87727-709-5.

Number 9 *Southeast Asian Capitalists*, ed. Ruth McVey. 1992. 2nd printing 1993. 220 pp. ISBN 0-87727-708-7.

Number 8 *The Politics of Colonial Exploitation: Java, the Dutch, and the Cultivation System*, Cornelis Fasseur, ed. R. E. Elson, trans. R. E. Elson, Ary Kraal. 1992. 2nd printing 1994. 266 pp. ISBN 0-87727-707-9.

Number 7 *A Malay Frontier: Unity and Duality in a Sumatran Kingdom*, Jane Drakard. 1990. 2nd printing 2003. 215 pp. ISBN 0-87727-706-0.

Number 6	*Trends in Khmer Art*, Jean Boisselier, ed. Natasha Eilenberg, trans. Natasha Eilenberg, Melvin Elliott. 1989. 124 pp., 24 plates. ISBN 0-87727-705-2.
Number 5	*Southeast Asian Ephemeris: Solar and Planetary Positions, A.D. 638–2000*, J. C. Eade. 1989. 175 pp. ISBN 0-87727-704-4.
Number 3	*Thai Radical Discourse: The Real Face of Thai Feudalism Today*, Craig J. Reynolds. 1987. 2nd printing 1994. 186 pp. ISBN 0-87727-702-8.
Number 1	*The Symbolism of the Stupa*, Adrian Snodgrass. 1985. Revised with index, 1988. 3rd printing 1998. 469 pp. ISBN 0-87727-700-1.

SEAP Series

Number 23	*Possessed by the Spirits: Mediumship in Contemporary Vietnamese Communities*. 2006. 186 pp. ISBN 0-877271-41-0 (pb).
Number 22	*The Industry of Marrying Europeans*, Vũ Trọng Phụng, trans. Thúy Tranviet. 2006. 66 pp. ISBN 0-877271-40-2 (pb).
Number 21	*Securing a Place: Small-Scale Artisans in Modern Indonesia*, Elizabeth Morrell. 2005. 220 pp. ISBN 0-877271-39-9.
Number 20	*Southern Vietnam under the Reign of Minh Mạng (1820-1841): Central Policies and Local Response*, Choi Byung Wook. 2004. 226pp. ISBN 0-0-877271-40-2.
Number 19	*Gender, Household, State: Đổi Mới in Việt Nam*, ed. Jayne Werner and Danièle Bélanger. 2002. 151 pp. ISBN 0-87727-137-2.
Number 18	*Culture and Power in Traditional Siamese Government*, Neil A. Englehart. 2001. 130 pp. ISBN 0-87727-135-6.
Number 17	*Gangsters, Democracy, and the State*, ed. Carl A. Trocki. 1998. Second printing, 2002. 94 pp. ISBN 0-87727-134-8.
Number 16	*Cutting across the Lands: An Annotated Bibliography on Natural Resource Management and Community Development in Indonesia, the Philippines, and Malaysia*, ed. Eveline Ferretti. 1997. 329 pp. ISBN 0-87727-133-X.
Number 15	*The Revolution Falters: The Left in Philippine Politics after 1986*, ed. Patricio N. Abinales. 1996. Second printing, 2002. 182 pp. ISBN 0-87727-132-1.
Number 14	*Being Kammu: My Village, My Life*, Damrong Tayanin. 1994. 138 pp., 22 tables, illus., maps. ISBN 0-87727-130-5.
Number 13	*The American War in Vietnam*, ed. Jayne Werner, David Hunt. 1993. 132 pp. ISBN 0-87727-131-3.
Number 12	*The Voice of Young Burma*, Aye Kyaw. 1993. 92 pp. ISBN 0-87727-129-1.
Number 11	*The Political Legacy of Aung San*, ed. Josef Silverstein. Revised edition 1993. 169 pp. ISBN 0-87727-128-3.
Number 10	*Studies on Vietnamese Language and Literature: A Preliminary Bibliography*, Nguyen Dinh Tham. 1992. 227 pp. ISBN 0-87727-127-5.
Number 8	*From PKI to the Comintern, 1924–1941: The Apprenticeship of the Malayan Communist Party*, Cheah Boon Kheng. 1992. 147 pp. ISBN 0-87727-125-9.
Number 7	*Intellectual Property and US Relations with Indonesia, Malaysia, Singapore, and Thailand*, Elisabeth Uphoff. 1991. 67 pp. ISBN 0-87727-124-0.

Number 6   *The Rise and Fall of the Communist Party of Burma (CPB)*, Bertil Lintner. 1990. 124 pp. 26 illus., 14 maps. ISBN 0-87727-123-2.

Number 5   *Japanese Relations with Vietnam: 1951–1987*, Masaya Shiraishi. 1990. 174 pp. ISBN 0-87727-122-4.

Number 3   *Postwar Vietnam: Dilemmas in Socialist Development*, ed. Christine White, David Marr. 1988. 2nd printing 1993. 260 pp. ISBN 0-87727-120-8.

Number 2   *The Dobama Movement in Burma (1930–1938)*, Khin Yi. 1988. 160 pp. ISBN 0-87727-118-6.

Cornell Modern Indonesia Project Publications

Number 75   *A Tour of Duty: Changing Patterns of Military Politics in Indonesia in the 1990s.* Douglas Kammen and Siddharth Chandra. 1999. 99 pp. ISBN 0-87763-049-6.

Number 74   *The Roots of Acehnese Rebellion 1989–1992*, Tim Kell. 1995. 103 pp. ISBN 0-87763-040-2.

Number 73   *"White Book" on the 1992 General Election in Indonesia*, trans. Dwight King. 1994. 72 pp. ISBN 0-87763-039-9.

Number 72   *Popular Indonesian Literature of the Qur'an*, Howard M. Federspiel. 1994. 170 pp. ISBN 0-87763-038-0.

Number 71   *A Javanese Memoir of Sumatra, 1945–1946: Love and Hatred in the Liberation War*, Takao Fusayama. 1993. 150 pp. ISBN 0-87763-037-2.

Number 70   *East Kalimantan: The Decline of a Commercial Aristocracy*, Burhan Magenda. 1991. 120 pp. ISBN 0-87763-036-4.

Number 69   *The Road to Madiun: The Indonesian Communist Uprising of 1948*, Elizabeth Ann Swift. 1989. 120 pp. ISBN 0-87763-035-6.

Number 68   *Intellectuals and Nationalism in Indonesia: A Study of the Following Recruited by Sutan Sjahrir in Occupation Jakarta*, J. D. Legge. 1988. 159 pp. ISBN 0-87763-034-8.

Number 67   *Indonesia Free: A Biography of Mohammad Hatta*, Mavis Rose. 1987. 252 pp. ISBN 0-87763-033-X.

Number 66   *Prisoners at Kota Cane*, Leon Salim, trans. Audrey Kahin. 1986. 112 pp. ISBN 0-87763-032-1.

Number 65   *The Kenpeitai in Java and Sumatra*, trans. Barbara G. Shimer, Guy Hobbs, intro. Theodore Friend. 1986. 80 pp. ISBN 0-87763-031-3.

Number 64   *Suharto and His Generals: Indonesia's Military Politics, 1975–1983*, David Jenkins. 1984. 4th printing 1997. 300 pp. ISBN 0-87763-030-5.

Number 62   *Interpreting Indonesian Politics: Thirteen Contributions to the Debate, 1964–1981*, ed. Benedict Anderson, Audrey Kahin, intro. Daniel S. Lev. 1982. 3rd printing 1991. 172 pp. ISBN 0-87763-028-3.

Number 60   *The Minangkabau Response to Dutch Colonial Rule in the Nineteenth Century*, Elizabeth E. Graves. 1981. 157 pp. ISBN 0-87763-000-3.

Number 59   *Breaking the Chains of Oppression of the Indonesian People: Defense Statement at His Trial on Charges of Insulting the Head of State, Bandung, June 7–10, 1979*, Heri Akhmadi. 1981. 201 pp. ISBN 0-87763-001-1.

Translation Series

Language Texts

INDONESIAN

Beginning Indonesian through Self-Instruction, John U. Wolff, Dédé Oetomo, Daniel Fietkiewicz. 3rd revised edition 1992. Vol. 1. 115 pp. ISBN 0-87727-529-7. Vol. 2. 434 pp. ISBN 0-87727-530-0. Vol. 3. 473 pp. ISBN 0-87727-531-9.

Indonesian Readings, John U. Wolff. 1978. 4th printing 1992. 480 pp. ISBN 0-87727-517-3

Indonesian Conversations, John U. Wolff. 1978. 3rd printing 1991. 297 pp. ISBN 0-87727-516-5

Formal Indonesian, John U. Wolff. 2nd revised edition 1986. 446 pp. ISBN 0-87727-515-7

TAGALOG

Pilipino through Self-Instruction, John U. Wolff, Maria Theresa C. Centeno, Der-Hwa V. Rau. 1991. Vol. 1. 342 pp. ISBN 0-87727—525-4. Vol. 2., revised 2005, 378 pp. ISBN 0-87727-526-2. Vol 3., revised 2005, 431 pp. ISBN 0-87727-527-0. Vol. 4. 306 pp. ISBN 0-87727-528-9.

THAI

A. U. A. Language Center Thai Course, J. Marvin Brown. Originally published by the American University Alumni Association Language Center, 1974. Reissued by Cornell Southeast Asia Program, 1991, 1992. Book 1. 267 pp. ISBN 0-87727-506-8. Book 2. 288 pp. ISBN 0-87727-507-6. Book 3. 247 pp. ISBN 0-87727-508-4.

A. U. A. Language Center Thai Course, Reading and Writing Text (mostly reading), 1979. Reissued 1997. 164 pp. ISBN 0-87727-511-4.

A. U. A. Language Center Thai Course, Reading and Writing Workbook (mostly writing), 1979. Reissued 1997. 99 pp. ISBN 0-87727-512-2.

KHMER

Cambodian System of Writing and Beginning Reader, Franklin E. Huffman. Originally published by Yale University Press, 1970. Reissued by Cornell Southeast Asia Program, 4th printing 2002. 365 pp. ISBN 0-300-01314-0.

Modern Spoken Cambodian, Franklin E. Huffman, assist. Charan Promchan, Chhom-Rak Thong Lambert. Originally published by Yale University Press, 1970. Reissued by Cornell Southeast Asia Program, 3rd printing 1991. 451 pp. ISBN 0-300-01316-7.

Intermediate Cambodian Reader, ed. Franklin E. Huffman, assist. Im Proum. Originally published by Yale University Press, 1972. Reissued by Cornell Southeast Asia Program, 1988. 499 pp. ISBN 0-300-01552-6.

Cambodian Literary Reader and Glossary, Franklin E. Huffman, Im Proum. Originally published by Yale University Press, 1977. Reissued by Cornell Southeast Asia Program, 1988. 494 pp. ISBN 0-300-02069-4.

HMONG

White Hmong-English Dictionary, Ernest E. Heimbach. 1969. 8th printing, 2002. 523 pp. ISBN 0-87727-075-9.

VIETNAMESE

Intermediate Spoken Vietnamese, Franklin E. Huffman, Tran Trong Hai. 1980. 3rd printing 1994. ISBN 0-87727-500-9.

* * *

Southeast Asian Studies: Reorientations. Craig J. Reynolds and Ruth McVey. Frank H. Golay Lectures 2 & 3. 70 pp. ISBN 0-87727-301-4.

Javanese Literature in Surakarta Manuscripts, Nancy K. Florida. Vol. 1, *Introduction and Manuscripts of the Karaton Surakarta*. 1993. 410 pp. Frontispiece, illustrations. Hard cover, ISBN 0-87727-602-1, Paperback, ISBN 0-87727-603-X. Vol. 2, *Manuscripts of the Mangkunagaran Palace*. 2000. 576 pp. Frontispiece, illustrations. Paperback, ISBN 0-87727-604-8.

Sbek Thom: Khmer Shadow Theater. Pech Tum Kravel, trans. Sos Kem, ed. Thavro Phim, Sos Kem, Martin Hatch. 1996. 363 pp., 153 photographs. ISBN 0-87727-620-X.

In the Mirror: Literature and Politics in Siam in the American Era, ed. Benedict R. O'G. Anderson, trans. Benedict R. O'G. Anderson, Ruchira Mendiones. 1985. 2nd printing 1991. 303 pp. Paperback. ISBN 974-210-380-1.

To order, please contact:

Cornell University
Southeast Asia Program Publications
95 Brown Road
Box 1004
Ithaca NY 14850

Online: http://www.einaudi.cornell.edu/southeastasia/publications/
Tel: 1-877-865-2432 (Toll free – U.S.)
Fax: (607) 255-7534

E-mail: SEAP-Pubs@cornell.edu
Orders must be prepaid by check or credit card (VISA, MasterCard, Discover).